PARTNERSHIPS
FOR
RURAL DEVELOPMENT

ORGANISATION FOR ECONOMIC CO-OPERATION AND DEVELOPMENT

Pursuant to article 1 of the Convention signed in Paris on 14th December 1960, and which came into force on 30th September 1961, the Organisation for Economic Co-operation and Development (OECD) shall promote policies designed:

- to achieve the highest sustainable economic growth and employment and a rising standard of living in Member countries, while maintaining financial stability, and thus to contribute to the development of the world economy;
- to contribute to sound economic expansion in Member as well as non-member countries in the process of economic development; and
- to contribute to the expansion of world trade on a multilateral, non-discriminatory basis in accordance with international obligations.

The original Member countries of the OECD are Austria, Belgium, Canada, Denmark, France, the Federal Republic of Germany, Greece, Iceland, Ireland, Italy, Luxembourg, the Netherlands, Norway, Portugal, Spain, Sweden, Switzerland, Turkey, the United Kingdom and the United States. The following countries became Members subsequently through accession at the dates indicated hereafter: Japan (28th April 1964), Finland (28th January 1969), Australia (7th June 1971) and New Zealand (29th May 1973).

The Socialist Federal Republic of Yugoslavia takes part in some of the work of the OECD (agreement of 28th October 1961).

Publié en français sous le titre:

**LES PARTENAIRES
POUR LE DÉVELOPPEMENT RURAL**

This study has been prepared by Christian Huillet and Pieter Van Dijk of the OECD Secretariat in assocation with Professor Theodore Alter, consultant. They were assisted by Michel Haas.

National experts on rural public management first discussed partnerships at their meeting in Athens, Greece, in May 1988 on Institutional Partnerships for Rural Policy Implementation. A draft of the present study was agreed by the same group at its meeting in Paris, October 1989. The Technical Co-operation Committee recommended its derestriction on the responsibility of the Secretary-General.

Also available

NEW TRENDS IN RURAL POLICYMAKING (1988)
(42 88 01 1) ISBN 92–64–13135–3 162 pp   £9.50   US$18.00   FF80   DM35

RURAL PUBLIC MANAGEMENT (1986)
(42 86 02 1) ISBN 92–64–12858–1 86 pp.   £5.00   US$10.00   FF50   DM25

RESTRUCTURING THE REGIONS. Analysis, Policy Model and Prognosis by
David Wadley (1986)
(70 86 03 1) ISBN 92–64–12868–9 172 pp.   £11.00   US$22.00   FF110   DM49

TABLE OF CONTENTS

Part II

PARTNERSHIPS FOR RURAL DEVELOPMENT
IN SELECTED COUNTRIES

INTRODUCTION

The OECD's work on rural public management began by illustrating how important and necessary it was for governments to redefine rural policy objectives, given the demographic, economic and socio–political trends in rural areas (OECD, 1986). It then sought to identify the institutional obstacles, and described a number of new institutional arrangements to overcome them (OECD, 1988).

One of the most striking issues in Member countries' recent efforts to address structural changes in rural areas is the trend towards more comprehensive, integrated policies. Such approaches necessarily bring together not only many sectoral departments, but also different levels of government and a wide spectrum of private sector economic and social interests. In many countries the ultimate viability of comprehensive rural policy–making is seen to depend on the capacities of a considerable number of heterogeneous institutions to work out together durable forms of co–operation that go beyond mutual consultations in the policy formulation phases, and provide for actual risk– and responsibility–sharing arrangements during the implementation phase. Partnership arrangements turned out to be the mechanism most countries had overall experience with, although the administrative, legal and political contexts vary widely within the Membership.

In some Member countries, use of partnership arrangements is embedded in constitutional law and political culture, and has a long tradition in policy implementation. In other Member countries, intergovernmental and public–private partnerships, with the sharing of authority, responsibility, and power that such arrangements entail, are relatively new phenomena. Those Member countries with considerable partnership experience have found them effective in varying degrees. These countries are seeking to innovate with new partnership arrangements in order to increase their effectiveness. Member countries with relatively little experience in the field are beginning to explore the organisational, managerial, and political parameters of partnership arrangements as mechanisms for rural policy implementation.

This report has two parts. Part I describes the organisational and policy aspects that are important for partnership machinery to operate. It presents information on various kinds of institutional partnerships, and the prospects they hold out for successful implementation of rural development programmes. Part II of the report summarises particular examples of institutional partnerships set up in OECD Member countries.

Part I

INSTITUTIONAL PARTNERSHIPS
FOR RURAL POLICY IMPLEMENTATION

Chapter I

RURAL CHANGE AND INSTITUTIONAL PARTNERSHIPS

During the last twenty years, rural areas[1] in most OECD Member countries have experienced numerous, often far–reaching economic, social and institutional changes. These changes have often had profound effects on the ways people in rural areas live, work and govern themselves. Today, the process of rural change continues, and it is posing significant challenges for the formulation and implementation of policy strategies to strengthen the socio–economic vitality of rural areas. This study focuses on the challenges of rural policy and programme implementation through partnership arrangements involving public and private sector actors[2].

Structural Change in Rural Areas

Rural areas have been affected significantly by social change. After a steady decline in the 1960s, population in rural areas grew in the 1970s, increasing significantly in some areas, often outpacing metropolitan population growth. Many people moving to rural areas came from urban and metropolitan settings seeking an improved living environment. During the 1980s, rural population growth slowed, and in some areas declined, in both absolute and relative terms compared to population in metropolitan areas. Demographic change increased, sometimes dramatically, the social and cultural diversity of many rural areas. One significant implication of this increased diversity was to expand the cultural and economic horizons of many rural people beyond their communities to include regional, national and international perspectives. Another significant implication was an increase in conflicts regarding interests, values and lifestyles.

Rural economies have become more diversified. Agriculture has continued to decline in importance, while the service sector has grown significantly. In some areas, small to medium–sized manufacturing enterprises have emerged as a source of employment, albeit in relatively low–wage activities, and an important part of the rural economic fabric. These enterprises, often owned and operated by local entrepreneurs, serve local, regional, national and sometimes international markets. Expansion of the leisure and tourism industry and the growth of some areas as retirement settlements have enhanced rural economic vitality.

Over the past few years, governments and society at large have come to realise that rural areas are the repository of much of the ecological resources, such as clean land, air and water, which are of major importance for the long–term needs of society and which form the basis for a sound biosphere. In many countries, rural landscapes and built–up areas have also come to be regarded as important parts of the cultural heritage which need to be protected and which require investments for their maintenance.

Institutional changes have also had a significant impact on the rural areas of many OECD countries. Two such changes, decentralisation of government and strengthening of the private and nonprofit sectors in rural areas, are especially important. Decentralisation has meant a greater role for regional and local governmental authorities in managing rural public affairs. It has also meant greater responsibilities and risks for decision–makers at those levels. The emergence of stronger private and nonprofit sectors has strengthened and enriched the social, economic and political fabric of many rural areas.

Institutional Challenges

Rural change has posed fundamental challenges for citizens, business and community leaders, and government officials concerned with the local and national importance of economically strong, environmentally sound and socially vibrant rural areas and communities. One challenge involves gaining a clear, current understanding of the socio–economic, environmental, and political problems important in rural areas. Another challenge involves identifying and developing feasible policy and programme strategies for addressing rural problems effectively. A third challenge is posed by the institutional context for formulating and implementing policies and programmes for addressing rural problems. The challenge in this case involves reorganising existing and designing new institutional arrangements to more effectively formulate and implement rural policies and programmes. While not in itself a guarantee of improvements in rural development, effective institutional arrangements are an important prerequisite for effective rural policies and programmes.

The social and economic changes that rural areas have experienced in recent years have helped alter perceptions of rural problems and of appropriate strategies to deal with these problems. Most OECD Member countries are now viewing rural problems from a more integrated, comprehensive perspective than in the past. Economic development, for example, is generally no longer viewed primarily or solely as a question of agricultural development. It is increasingly recognised that other factors, such as investment and industrial strategies, employment policies, education, health and social services, housing and transportation facilities, are interdependent, and affect each other as well as agriculture in the development of rural economies and communities. This integrated, comprehensive view of rural problems has, in turn, affected perceptions of appropriate policy and programme strategies. Most Member countries recognise that rural development policy and programme strategies must be grounded in a global — not a piecemeal, problem–by–problem — perspective on rural areas and issues. Effective policy and programme strategies must be comprehensive and address issues in an integrated fashion.

Recent developments indicate that Member countries are also addressing the institutional challenges posed by rural change and the need for an integrated, global approach to rural policy–making. With respect to the institutional context, certain common tendencies appear to be emerging in the Member countries, despite differences in governmental traditions and political cultures. These tendencies include:

— an increase in the array of interests being encouraged to participate and actually participating in the process of formulating rural policies and programmes at all levels of government;
— changes in the distribution of policy formulation responsibilities among government ministries and departments that reflect recognition of the importance of an integrated global approach to rural policy–making;
— recognition that decentralisation of government authority and responsibility alone is not sufficient to rectify institutional rigidities hindering the formulation of integrated, global rural policies; and
— growing co–operation between public and private sector decisionmakers in defining and seeking solutions to rural development problems.

The critical importance of institutional arrangements for implementing policies and programmes is often slighted relative to concerns with understanding issues and formulating policy and programme strategies. Effective implementation is fundamental to effective policy and programme performance. Implementation is the process of putting public policies and programmes into action. Theoretically sound, properly designed and appropriately targeted public policies and programmes with broad political support from multiple interests are not likely to achieve their full potential, and may well fail completely, if the organisational, managerial and political requisites for effective implementation are not in place. Based on their experience with rural problems and policies in recent years, Member countries are well aware that the implementation process and the institutional arrangements that frame that process have an important impact on rural policy performance. As a consequence, they have been seeking more effective approaches for rural policy implementation.

Partnerships for Rural Policy Implementation

In responding to the challenge of more effectively implementing rural policies and programmes, governments in many OECD Member countries are actively pursuing various types of institutional partnership arrangements. These partnerships may involve different levels of government, sectoral ministries, government agencies, private business, professional associations, community voluntary organisations and other interests. While not seen as a panacea for solving rural development problems, partnerships are thought to be effective instruments for improving relationships among public agencies, levels of government and private sector organisations, and for combining human and financial resources from a variety of sources for achieving rural policy objectives. They often result in innovative organisational designs which can enhance managerial competence and the exercise of political authority. Partnerships appear to offer a mechanism for bonding together the multiple interests and perspectives necessary to implement integrated, global policy and programme strategies responsive to diverse local socio–economic conditions in rural areas.

OECD Member country interest in institutional partnerships for rural policy implementation seems to be grounded mainly in the context and political economy of rural policy–making. From a policy perspective, institutional partnerships:

i) can be mechanisms for merging the objectives, experiences and resources of multiple institutional and individual actors necessarily involved in an integrated, territorial approach to rural policy;

ii) if properly structured, are capable of providing the flexibility necessary to identify and to respond more efficiently and effectively to the diverse local socio–economic and political circumstances of rural areas;

iii) can help organise and enhance complementarity of rural development programme purpose vertically among levels of government and horizontally across governmental units at the same level; and

iv) can provide a means to organise and to capitalise on the advantages of pragmatic public and private sector co–operation.

Rural development in Canada is a shared responsibility of several levels of government: national, provincial, local and community. Because the division of powers between levels of government is an evolving phenomenon based on constitutional interpretation and custom, rural development policy varies among the partners concerned. Given the complex nature of the challenge faced by rural areas, it is quite clear that there is often a need for co–operation and co–ordination within and among levels of government. Two types of partnerships have been developed: horizontal arrangements among parts of the administration at the same level, and vertical arrangements among different levels of government. Both types of partnerships were put in place to enhance the development prospects of aboriginal communities in the Province of Québec, most of which are rural and isolated.

The use of institutional partnerships among public sector and public and private sector actors designed to achieve public policy objectives is in general not a new phenomenon. Historically, such partnerships have been used to achieve a variety of public purposes, including rural development, to varying degrees in most OECD Member countries. Some Member countries appear to have used institutional partnership arrangements in formulating and implementing public policies and programmes more than others. In general, those countries with more decentralised systems of government, such as the Federal Republic of Germany and the United States, seem to have had relatively more experience with public and private sector partnerships than countries with more centralised, unitary systems, such as France and Greece. This generalisation, however, does not always hold. Both the Netherlands and the United Kingdom, countries with unitary systems, have traditionally relied upon public and public–private partnerships for implementing as well as formulating public policies, including rural policies. Thus it appears that Member country experience with institutional partnerships has some basis in problem–solving expediency and administrative tradition as well as the constitutional context of government.

NOTES AND REFERENCES

1. In this report, the term "rural" is used in its geographical sense. It covers regions having scattered activities and includes villages, towns, regional centres and industrialised rural areas. However, it excludes peri-urban areas situated in the economic and administrative orbit of a metropolitan area.

2. In this report, the term "public sector" refers to all the administrations and administrative agents of the government, whether central or decentralised, as well as the services and civil servants of regional and local collectivities. As opposed to the public sector, the private sector designates the totality of the enterprises and socio-cultural associations who are rural development actors.

Chapter II

PERSPECTIVES ON INSTITUTIONAL PARTNERSHIPS

Interest in Partnerships

Member country experiences in dealing with rural public management issues have repeatedly shown that the effectiveness of public policies and programmes depends to a large extent on the institutional arrangements for implementing them. For rural development policies, which increasingly cut across traditional sectors of society and governmental jurisdictions, partnership arrangements among public and private sector institutions are receiving more and more attention as mechanisms for policy implementation. Member countries are using these various partnership arrangements to carry out policies and programmes focusing on a broad array of rural development issues, including business development and job creation, water resource management, manpower training and education and public service delivery.

These institutional partnerships, designed to carry out comprehensive policies to address the problems and opportunities posed by structural adjustments in rural areas, involve different levels of government; related ministries at the same level of government; independent public enterprises such as transportation, water supply and housing authorities; and private sector organisations. Private sector organisations include industries, banks, professional associations, voluntary community organisations, and interest groups organised to pursue specific societal goals. Examples of such partnerships are operational in almost all Member countries.

While institutional partnerships are not a new phenomenon in public management, the process of implementing comprehensive, multi–sectoral rural structural adjustment policies has raised several important organisational, managerial and political issues that have caused a reexamination of existing partnership arrangements and an interest in developing new partnerships. At the central government level, for example, the issue of making decisions and allocating resources based on a multi–sectoral perspective has focused on interministerial co–ordination as a key element in rural policy implementation. Such co–ordination is necessary to marshall more effectively financial and other resources to support rural policies and programmes based on an integrated, global perspective.

For some Member countries, regional or local governments have become significant, perhaps the most significant, partners in rural policy formulation and implementation. Rural development policy–making responsibility and authority has been decentralised to the regional or local level. This phenomenon acknowledges that decision–makers at sub–national levels are often better positioned to identify problems and to design and implement appropriate policies to alleviate these problems than are decision–makers at the central level. Such decentralisation of policy–making responsibility, however, may not be accompanied by delegation of commensurate budgetary and legal authority. As a consequence, for institutional partnerships grounded in a prominent role for regional or local government to be effective, innovative approaches must be found to strengthen relationships among regional governments and their central and local government, and perhaps private sector, partners.

In the United Kingdom, the Rural Development Commission is the principal agency for carrying forward the Government's rural development policies and programmes in England. The Commission works in partnership with a wide range of governmental, community, and private sector agencies and organisations in pursuing this goal. The Rural Development Commission is one example among the many institutional partnerships involving central government departments and agencies, local governments, private sector enterprises and community voluntary organisations for implementing rural policies and programmes in the United Kingdom. Its institutional history dates back to 1909 and over the years many changes have occurred in the objectives, structures and types of partnerships involved, reflecting both the changing nature of rural problems and policy responses.

Historically, private actors have played an important role in the economic and social development of rural areas. The independence, initiative and innovation of local entrepreneurs, firms and voluntary organisations has contributed significantly to the economic well–being, public service base and overall quality of life in many rural communities. These private sector actors, however, are dependent on government. Government provides the macro–economic environment and the legal and administrative framework for local economic, public service and environmental initiatives. Given this context, Member countries are turning increasingly to various forms of public–private co–operation and partnership for implementing rural development policies. Such partnerships are viewed as effective mechanisms for combining public and private sector resources and for directing those resources toward the solution of important rural problems.

Types of Partnerships

The notion of institutional partnerships is broad. Institutional partnerships can take many forms, can be used for many purposes, and involve complex legal, political, organisational and financial interrelationships among partners. The essence of any partnership, however, is an orchestration of policy and execution, based on shared objectives and priorities. In the context of this study, partnerships are systems of formalized co–operation, grounded in legally binding arrangements or informal understandings, co–operative working relationships, and mutually adopted plans among a

18

number of institutions. They involve agreements on policy and programme objectives and the sharing of responsibility, resources, risks and benefits over a specified period of time.

Institutional partnerships involve two key dimensions: a policy dimension and an operational dimension. Within the policy dimension, partnership objectives are articulated; within the operational dimension, these objectives are pursued. The policy dimension involves processes that result in agreement on objectives, roles and responsibilities of partners and provide the basis for sustained political support for partnership activities. The broader and more far-reaching the partnership objectives and the more multi-faceted and complex the partnership working relationships, the more important is the underlying political foundation for the partnership arrangement. The operational dimension involves the management tasks of specifying working relationships among partners, structuring decision-making procedures, determining procedures and criteria for marshalling and allocating resources, and carrying out other activities necessary to implement partnership policies and programmes.

Institutional partnerships for rural policy implementation can be characterised along several different dimensions including their purpose, institutional form, scale and nature of partnership agreement. In Member countries, the purposes addressed by an institutional partnership may be very broadly or very narrowly defined. The Amvrakikos Gulf planning contract in Greece, for example, is designed to address the full scope of economic, environmental, infrastructural and social needs associated with integrated rural development. In contrast, the Rural Occupations Experiment in Finland focuses on rural employment generation, and the Job Training Partnership Act in the United States focuses on cyclical and structural unemployment.

With regard to institutional form, institutional partnerships for rural policy implementation are of two general types: public sector partnerships and public-private sector partnerships. Public sector partnerships may be intergovernmental partnerships or intragovernmental partnerships. Intergovernmental partnerships include co-operative working agreements among levels of government, or among central, regional and local or communal governments. Intergovernmental partnerships also include working agreements among governmental jurisdictions at the same level. Intragovernmental partnerships involve co-operative working arrangements among ministries, agencies and other similar entities at the same level of government. Many public sector partnerships involve both inter- and intragovernmental partnerships.

Public-private sector partnerships involve co-operation among individuals and organisations in the public and private sectors for mutual benefit. Public-private partnerships are often government-business partnerships, but they are not limited to business and government. In addition to business, private partners might include non-profit organisations such as schools and universities, hospitals, community development and community service organisations, and co-operatives. Private partners might also include professional associations, neighbourhood associations, voluntary organisations, religious institutions, families and individuals.

The terms "public-private partnership" and "privatisation" are sometimes used almost synonymously. Public-private partnerships do, in fact, involve elements of privatisation, such as the substantial involvement of private sector organisations in the planning, financing, production and delivery of public goods and services through public policies and programmes. They do not, however, include privatisation in the sense that government delegates all responsibility for public goods provision, production and delivery to the private sector.

The General Directorate of Rural Affairs (GDRA) in Turkey is a partnership of central and provincial organisations, designed to facilitate implementation of a multisectoral rural development policy. The GDRA is affiliated financially and legally with the Ministry of Agriculture, Forestry and Rural Affairs. The GDRA brings together the main resource departments at the central government level most important for rural development, such as the planning, land and housing, irrigation, village drinking water, and village electrification departments. It also involves representatives from appropriate advisory and support service units. The GDRA is represented at the regional and provincial levels by 18 regional directorates and 67 provincial directorates. The GDRA is a tool to assist the central government in developing co–operation and co–ordination among central, regional, and provincial government administrations and other organisations involved with rural development issues.

In addition to their purposes and institutional form, partnerships for rural policy implementation can be characterised according to their scale. The scale of some partnerships is very large, while the scale of other partnerships may be quite small. Cooperative Extension in the United States, for example, is a partnership of federal, state and local government and citizens designed to provide research–based information and education to farmers, local leaders, community groups, households, young people and others that help these people address the economic, environmental and social issues they face. Cooperative Extension has an organised presence in every county in the United States. In contrast, the local development programme of Motril, a rural municipality in southern Spain, involves a relatively small–scale partnership arrangement designed to strengthen the economy of the Motril and the surrounding local area.

Finally, partnerships can be characterised by the nature of the partnership agreement. Agreements can range in form from legally–binding to loosely–structured, more informal political agreements.

Role of Partnerships

All public policies and programmes are designed to address two core public sector functions: the provision of public goods and the production of public goods. Institutional partnerships are mechanisms for linking these core functions. Public goods involve activities with effects or outcomes that accrue to groups of people or society as a whole. They must be provided through some type of governmental or other collective action because of the high level of risk associated with them, their large scale and resource requirements, and the lack of incentive or capacity for individuals or organisations to voluntarily provide the goods themselves. Examples of traditional broad categories of public goods include education, environmental quality, economic development, highways and public transportation, national defence, and social welfare assistance for individuals and families.

Government plays an important role in organising the provision of public goods. It must decide what to provide, how to pay for it and how to produce it. Government does not, however, necessarily have to play a role in organising public goods production. Distinguishing public goods provision from public goods production suggests a range of institutional arrangements for linking the two functions. The traditional arrangement involves a single unit of government organising both the provision and production of public goods. Roads, drinking–water supply, and waste water treatment are examples of public goods that have traditionally and primarily been the sole responsibility of local or communal governments in many OECD Member countries.

Village renewal is important for enhancing the social and economic development of rural areas in Germany. The supply of jobs in commercial and industrical enterprises can be stabilised through village renewal, and the attractiveness of villages and rural areas can also be increased.

Village renewal efforts are grounded in a financial partnership between communes, federal government administration and *Länder* governments. This partnership allows the federal government to support rural development in accordance with the spatial and technical guidelines established by the *Länder* and communes.

Specifically, village renewal involves improving the identity of communes and villages as rural settlements by carrying out measures aimed at bringing out the distinctive character of the townscape. It is provided for in an amendment of the Urban Development Assistance Act introduced on 1st January 1985. Village renewal measures provide assistance in the fields of water management and construction technology for cultural buildings and individual enterprises as well as on the re–allocation and consolidation of agricultural land holdings, the voluntary exchange of land, and coastal protection.

Another set of institutional arrangements involves partnerships for addressing the basic problems of organising public economies. Public sector partnerships involving intergovernmental or intragovernmental co–operation might be used to address the provision question, the production question or both questions. With respect to public goods production, for example, governmental units might co–operate to produce public goods through joint production or intergovernmental contracting. In a joint production arrangement, two or more provision units jointly organise a single production unit. In an intergovernmental contracting arrangement, one unit of local government assumes responsibility for organising provision but contracts production to another governmental unit. Contractual policy in France and Greece are examples of intergovernmental partnerships where all governmental partners are involved in both provision and production.

Since 1988 the French Ministry of Agriculture and Forestry has been experimenting with a new approach to rural development, to redefine the bounds of the intercommunal planning and development charters whose area was too limited. The approach now is to identify local potential to compete with other regions, with the help of a consultancy firm, and then to implement selective programming. The new approach entails close co-operation, within "piloting committees", between the various tiers of government, local councils and the economic actors concerned. The partners — representatives of central government (the prefect, directors of external services), the local authorities (mayors, general and regional counsellors) and trade and professional organisations — draw up a selective list of significant projects to be given priority and set in place the structures and people needed to run them. This approach ensures that all the agents work together consistently, and promotes an intersectoral policy of rural development.

Public–private partnerships, like public sector partnerships, encompass a range of institutional alternatives for addressing the key questions of providing and producing public goods in a public economy. Through public–private partnerships, both partners may deal jointly with provision and production, or the public partner(s) may address provision and engage private partners to deal with production. Such partnerships include those organisational arrangements referred to as quangos[1], parastatals and paragovernmentals. One rationale sometimes given for public–private partnerships, particularly those that engage private sector partners in producing public goods, is that the motivation of private sector partners to minimise costs and improve programme performance may result in better, more cost–effective government programmes. Public–private sector partnerships have been used in Ireland, the United States, and other OECD Member countries for purposes such as providing public services, building human capital and fostering economic development.

NOTES AND REFERENCES

1. Quangos: quasi–autonomous, non–governmental organisations: independent administrative services who are linked, nonetheless, by their object or by their structure, to the government administration.

Chapter III

RATIONALE FOR INSTITUTIONAL PARTNERSHIPS

Historically, institutional partnerships have been used to a varying extent for various purposes ranging from managing urban services to environmental protection to rural electrification by numerous OECD Member countries. In recent years, many Member countries have given increased attention to partnership arrangements for formulating and implementing public policies and programmes in rural areas. While the pragmatic administrative, legal and political reasons for this increased attention vary from country to country, several additional important justifications are grounded in the context and political economy of rural policy–making.

The Rural Policy–making Context

Three dimensions of the rural policy–making context provide important reasons for Member country interest in partnership arrangements for implementing rural policies. These dimensions are the emerging broad scope of rural policy, the inherent socio–economic characteristics and conditions of rural areas, and the complex, changing institutional environment within which rural policies and programmes are formulated and implemented.

The Broad Scope of Rural Policy

Many OECD Member countries are moving toward a more global, integrated perspective on rural policy. It is increasingly being recognised and accepted that development in rural areas is not just a sectoral problem, involving agriculture, manufacturing or services, and that it is not simply a question of economics. A view is emerging that it is constructive to view rural development as a broad notion, encompassing all important issues pertinent to the individual and collective vitality of rural people and places. It encompasses such concerns as education, environment, individual and public health, housing, public services and facilities, capacity for leadership and governance, and cultural heritage as well as sectorial and general economic issues. In effect, this view reflects a spatial or territorial as opposed to a sectorial approach to rural development.

The emergence of this spatial or territorial approach has two important implications for rural policy–making. First, under this approach, rural policy involves more than just economic growth; instead, it involves the broad range of development issues and concerns related to the socio–economic vitality of rural people and rural areas. Second, since rural policy under this view encompasses such a broad range of concerns, it necessarily affects many different governmental and private sector actors.

This broad perspective on rural policy, involving many actors, poses an important institutional challenge. The challenge is how best to bring these multiple actors with their varying interests, experiences, and resources together in a co–operative and co–ordinated fashion to deal effectively with rural issues.

The UK Rural Development Commission's two main efforts involve providing support for rural economic enterprise development and ensuring development and improvement of public services and facilities in rural communities. In pursuing these goals, the Rural Development Commission works in partnership with a wide array of central government departments and agencies, local governments, private sector enterprises and community voluntary organisations. These partnerships help ensure that 1) available skills and resources are used to the best advantage; 2) the ideas of local people and their knowledge of local socio–economic conditions is utilised and reflected in national rural development programmes; 3) the private sector and local interest groups are involved in implementing the Government's rural development policies and programmes; 4) private sector development and local enterprise are encouraged and the need for public sector intervention reduced.

Characteristics of Rural Areas

Certain fundamental characteristics common to most rural areas have important implications for rural public management. These characteristics suggest the need for flexibility in the design and operation of institutional arrangements and procedures for formulating and implementing rural policies and programmes.

The most fundamental characteristic of rural areas in this regard is their diversity. This diversity manifests itself along many dimensions. Rural areas are diverse in terms of the quantity and quality of human, capital and natural resources available to support socio–economic development. Some rural areas have actually achieved relatively high levels of development, while other areas are underdeveloped relative to their potential.

In addition to their diversity, rural areas are characterised by several additional factors that have important implications for implementing rural policies and programmes. Many rural areas tend to have relatively small populations and, in most areas, this population is dispersed over the countryside instead of being concentrated in villages or towns of significant size. In addition, many rural areas are relatively isolated spatially as well as socio–economically and politically from major urban and metropolitan areas and centres of government. Furthermore, strong individual and collective capacity for leadership and governance in many rural communities is often lacking. Together, these factors merge to increase the organisational difficulties and costs of implementing government programmes and delivering public services in rural areas relative to more densely populated, less isolated areas.

French communes are small, with limited administrative capacity and low budgets; these factors make any real economic development policy hard to implement at the commune level. Rural development thus calls for a broader approach, across a number of communes, through the Intercommunal Planning and Development Charters. This mechanism was created in 1982 following the "Plans d'Aménagement rural" and the "Contrats de pays" which have existed since the 1970s. These charters, which are action programmes prepared and endorsed by the local authorities, cover a range of matters — economic (housing, training, agriculture, physical planning, etc.) and socio–cultural (leisure activities). Based on genuine solidarity among local authorities, they very frequently involve trade and professional groups and voluntary organisations, strong factors in development, and are prepared with the assistance of the département and the region. As the areas covered have proved too small and the organisational structures somewhat limited, however, the intercommunal charters have now been superseded by rural development programmes encompassing larger areas under a new strategic approach. This change was initiated by the French central government in the framework of the 1989–93 "Contrats de plan" signed with the regional governments.

Diversity of socio–economic conditions and development potentials; small, dispersed populations; spatial and political isolation; and insufficient leadership and governance capacities pose special rural public management challenges. Institutional arrangements for formulating and implementing rural policies and programmes must be sensitive to these characteristics, and they must be flexible enough to accomodate the wide diversity of rural conditions and problems and their change over time. Partnership arrangements of various types are currently being viewed by many OECD Member countries as institutional structures that provide the sensitivity and flexibility necessary for more effective implementation of rural policies and programmes.

Institutional Environment

Several changes in the institutional environment for formulating and implementing rural policies and programmes are especially significant. First, the trend in many Member countries towards a global, territorial approach to rural policy encompassing a range of sectorial policy concerns brings together many public and private sector actors. At the central government level, a territorial policy approach has by necessity involved merging the efforts of numerous ministries with pertinent expertise, such as those dealing with agriculture, environment, industry and commerce, labour, education, and health and human affairs.

The structure and nature of intergovernmental relations are key components of the complex institutional environment for formulating and implementing rural policies and programmes. In most Member countries, responsibility for rural issues and policies is shared to varying degrees among central, regional and local levels of government. In addition, at each of these levels, agencies of central government ministries with responsibilities for rural issues are likely to be involved in helping regional and local authorities. For European Community members, an additional dimension of this intergovernmental picture is the rural initiatives of the EC[1]. Central, regional, and local governments in EC countries may well be affected by and thus have a stake in these initiatives.

The second critical change affecting the institutional environment for rural public management is the decentralisation of decision–making and programme management authority and responsibility that has occured in recent years in most OECD Member countries. This shift in roles and responsibilities has altered the nature and pattern of intergovernmental relations with respect to rural as well as other policy issues in these countries. It has caused all levels of government to rethink how they can best work together to formulate and implement policies and programmes. The shift has also caused regional and local governments, particularly, to examine closely this administrative, financial and managerial capacities to carry out their responsibilities effectively.

Greece is experimenting with contractual policy, specifically planning and development contracts, as a mechanism for implementing as well as formulating rural development policies and programmes. Planning and development contracts are institutional partnerships designed to enhance participation at all levels of an ever–increasing range of representative agencies of the population. Simply stated, these contracts involve mutual agreement among central and local government and private sector partners regarding the distribution and interdependence of responsibilities for formulating, financing and implementing rural development initiatives. They provide flexibility necessary to tailor rural policies and programmes to the particular development needs and advantages of different rural areas. The Amvrakikos Gulf area, a typical example of a rural area that, up to now, underutilised and neglected its development potential, was the first major pilot project involving the planning contract approach. The Amvrakikos Planning Contract, initiated in 1985, involves close co–operation and co–ordination among central government and local authorities and interests. It places a premium on local self–reliance and involves decentralisation of responsiblity and authority for formulating and implementing development policies and programmes.

A third important change in the institutional environment for implementing rural policies involves changes in the nature of public and private sector interactions. In many OECD Member countries, there has been a growing pragmatic co–operation between the public and private sector, where the traditional boundaries between roles and responsibilities no longer strictly apply. In effect, numerous Member countries have been considering, and actively initiating, increased roles and responsibilities for the private sector in implementing rural policies and programmes. In some Member countries, for example, private sector organisations and enterprises have worked co-operatively with government agencies in implementing economic development initiatives and in producing and delivering local public services. Involving private actors in policy and programme implementation has potential in some situations for increasing the cost effectiveness of governmental activities.

The Town Council of Motril, Spain, a municipality in a rural area on the coast of Granada Province, has launched a development programme designed to strengthen the local economy. This local development programme has been initiated by a partnership of local and regional government and private sector actors. At the local level, enterpreneurs, labour unions, chambers of commerce and financial institutions have worked with the Town Council in formulating and implementing this programme. These partners have collaborated in carrying out various programme projects, including building a new hospital, creating two fishing co-operatives and establishing a company for managing rural services. Regional government also plays an important partnership role through the funding it provides to support the programme's activities. The Motril local development programme is designed to assist the local economy in achieving more fully its economic potential.

The complex, changing institutional environment for rural policy and programme implementation in most OECD Member countries is causing these countries to rethink their implementation strategies. The primary characteristic of this institutional environment is the vast array and diversity of actors with a stake in rural issues. A fundamental concern for Member countries is how best to involve and organise these actors so that they can co-operatively work together as partners in focusing their resources, experiences and capacities on solutions to rural problems. In dealing with this concern, many Member countries have been examining new as well as existing partnership arrangements involving governmental agencies and units and public and private sector actors.

The Political Economy of Institutional Partnerships

Another rationale for institutional partnerships for rural policy-making is grounded in the incentives for individual actors to participate as partners in the context of rural policy-making. The rationale inherent in the emerging global, territorial approach to rural policy, the characteristics of rural areas, and the institutional context of rural public management suggest why institutional partnerships as mechanisms for rural policy formulation and implementation seem sensible to many OECD Member countries. Effective, co-operative partnerships will not normally emerge and function, however, unless those actors who may become partners have specific individual incentives to participate. The collective local, regional and national importance of societal change, such as the enhanced socio–economic vitality of rural areas, often will not provide totally adequate incentives for individual actors to participate fully and co–operatively in a partnership arrangement. The possible incentives for different actors to participate in partnership arrangements are numerous. These incentives constitute a set of micro–level reasons why institutional partnerships are receiving renewed attention as appropriate mechanisms for rural policy and programme implementation in many Member countries.

Public Sector Perspectives

Partnership arrangements for rural policy implementation have several pragmatic, operational advantages for governments. First, partnership arrangements can provide governments at various levels with access to a regular flow of current, detailed information about the changing and diverse local circumstances in rural areas. The greater the involvement of public and private sector actors who deal directly with the people and problems of these areas on a daily basis, the greater the advantage of the partnership arrangement in this regard. The possibility of involving public and private actors with detailed knowledge of conditions in rural areas in the policy implementation process thus provides a second important reason why institutional partnership arrangements may have appeal for governments. A third advantage of partnerships for governments is that such arrangements provide a mechanism for organising and mobilising a range of resources, experiences and capacities from multiple partners, thus augmenting and enriching the mix of resources that can be effectively targeted on the needs and problems of rural people and areas.

Partnership arrangements appear also to have political advantages for governments. Through the involvement of multiple partners, they may provide a means to broaden political support for important governmental rural policy goals and initiatives. Further, partnerships may be viewed positively by some governments as appropriate mechanisms for furthering the democratic ideal of broader participation in collective decision–making and action regarding rural and other important public issues.

The Job Training Partnership Act (JTPA) has helped in fostering job training programmes to address cyclical and structural unemployment problems in rural areas as well as other parts of the United States. The JTPA is grounded in a complex matrix of partnership relationships among federal, state and local governments and among government and private sector actors. Much of the responsibility for implementation of the JTPA rests with a partnership of public and private sector actors at the local sub–state level, with the private sector partners playing a significant role in the partnership. The purpose of the JTPA is to provide job training programmes to economically disadvantaged and dislocated workers. Its organisation and operation is based on the decentralisation of governmental authority for job training from federal to state and local governments, a central feature of current federal job training policy in the United States.

> The Australian Country Centres Project (CCP) was a pilot initiative of the central Government's 1986 Rural Economic Package. The project was conducted in eleven rural centres suffering the cumulative socio–economic pressures of rural industrial decline.
>
> Specifically, the purpose of the CCP was to determine whether:
>
> — Local economies have the potential to make a greater contribution to the aggregate performance of the national economy;
> — Local communities have the capability to develop self–help strategies to identify and realise opportunities to facilitate economic regeneration and adjustment; and
> — An appropriate management and organisational framework could be established, with the co–ordinated assistance of all levels of government, to support local development.
>
> Broad–based liaison committees, comprising representatives of business, local goverment and the community, were established in each of the eleven centres to manage the project at the local level. The central government provided overall management and co–ordination, gave technical advice and information, and undertook overall monitoring and dissemination of results. State governments provided advice on the selection of regions, participated in liaison commmittees, and assisted the central government in evaluating the outcomes of the project.
>
> The CCP approach offers considerable promise for meeting community and national growth and adjustment objectives and enhancing the effectiveness of Government programmes at the local level.

Private Sector Perspectives

Institutional partnership arrangements also are likely to offer certain advantages to individual private sector partners, thus providing incentives for their participation. The pursuit of a collective rural policy goal, such as economic development, may well be consistent with the individual personal goals of private partners. Economic development and growth of a rural area, for example, may improve the economic position and expand the economic opportunities of specific actors or groups of actors represented in a partnership arrangement. Participation in a partnership arrangement may also increase access to information and a broader set of political and social contacts, which may help further the interests of particular private partners. A third aspect of institutional partnerships that may be attractive to private sector partners is the opportunity partnerships afford to pool and spread the financial and political risks of undertaking large–scale rural development efforts with uncertain payoffs with other partners, from both the private and public sectors. Public sector partners are likely to view this dimension of partnerships favourably as well. Finally, partnership arrangements provide private sector actors with an official forum for participating in the process of setting and carrying out the rural policy agenda. Through this forum, private sector actors may be able to articulate their perspectives and possibly influence the policy agenda more effectively than if they were not participants in a partnership arrangement.

NOTE AND REFERENCE

1. See chapter on the Commission the the European Communities.

Chapter IV

INSTITUTIONAL PARTNERSHIPS
AND POLICY IMPLEMENTATION

For institutional partnerships to be effective mechanisms for rural policy implementation, their organisation and operation must be sensitive to and accomodate the important attributes of the implementation process. In this section, several of these important attributes are detailed.

The Policy–making Process

Public policy–making is a complex, dynamic process involving continuing efforts to determine what should and can be done to resolve societal problems. Viewed simply, the public policy–making process consists of five basic elements or phases: problem identification, policy formulation, policy and programme implementation, evaluation and feedback, and policy and programme termination. Public problem identification occurs when societal needs that cannot be met through private action alone are perceived, clearly articulated or defined, and placed on the public policy agenda. Policy formulation is the process of establishing policy goals and developing general policy strategies as well as specific programme initiatives to achieve those goals. Implementation involves putting public policies and programmes into action. Evaluation and feedback involves monitoring the performance of programme initiatives and changes in societal needs and feeding the resulting information back into the previous stages of the public policy–making process. Policy and programme termination involves eliminating public policies and programmes that are ineffective or no longer useful or feasible.

All phases of the public policy–making process are interrelated and important in shaping public policy. Each phase involves continuation of the complex, dynamic and cyclical process of interaction, bargaining and negotiation which characterises public policy–making. Public policy thus emerges as the policy process plays itself out through each phase over time. Public policy is not just a reflection of the goals and strategies articulated during the policy formulation phase; it is also shaped by the interaction, bargaining, and negotiation among public and private sector actors that occurs during the implementation and other phases of the policy–making process.

31

Ireland is experimenting with a novel integrated rural development programme. The principle underlying this programme is that economic development in rural communities and areas should reflect the ideas and be a responsibility of local people. The programme calls for a Core Group, a partnership of community group representatives, local leaders and other individuals, to assume this responsibility for local development areas. Through this programme, Ireland hopes to revive and strengthen its rural areas, and thus enhance the social and economic well—being of the nation as a whole.

Implementation includes all activities necessary to put policies and programmes into action. These activities include interpretation, organisation and application. Interpretation is the process of translating policy and programme language into directives for action that are acceptable and feasible. Organisation involves establishing the institutional structures and operating procedures for marshalling and handling resources and putting a programme into action. Application involves the actual delivery of public programmes to specified people and places.

Effective implementation is fundamental to effective policy and programme performance. Effective implementation is necessary but not sufficient for achieving desired policy and programme performance. While effective implementation may not ensure that policy and programme goals are achieved, ineffective implementation almost always ensures that goals will not be achieved.

The Integrated Regional Development Programmes (PIRD) in Portugal are a regional policy initiative of the Ministry of Planning and Territorial Administration for comprehensive development of rural areas. Each programme is prepared on a partnership basis by the Programme Co—ordinating Council, whose members represent local and regional government services, local councils, employers' associations and trade unions, environmental pressure groups and cultural associations. At full meetings or in its committees, the Co—ordinating Council appraises the situation in the area, identifies bottlenecks, evaluates potentials and defines targets and actions to be taken. The central government intervenes only to ensure that the development programme is compatible with its own economic and social policy.

Aspects of Policy Implementation

The process of implementing public policies and programmes can be viewed from several different perspectives. Taken together, these perspectives reflect the complexity and dynamism of implementation, and they detail a number of critical realities that should be considered in designing the institutional arrangements and developing strategies for policy and programme implementation. These perspectives are:

- implementation as evolution;
- implementation as planning, hierarchy and control;
- implementation as politics; and
- implementation as a combination of statutory structures, problem tractability and nonstatutory forces.

Implementation as evolution reflects the notion that once public policy is formulated, it is reformulated during the implementation process. Policy that emerges from the formulation phase of the policy–making process incorporates policymakers' ideas, goals and dispositions regarding desired courses of action to help resolve important societal problems. During this phase, it is not possible to foresee all of the political, organisational and technical factors that may foster or inhibit moving in these directions once a policy is adopted. These unforeseen factors become evident during implementation, and as they are dealt with, a policy evolves from its original conception to one that reflects the influence of these factors. In addition, decisions are made during implementation about which of a policy's several objectives to pursue, in what order, and with what level of resource commitment.

Implementation as planning, hierarchy and control is grounded in the idea that implementation must ensure desired policy goals and performance as specified in legislation. From this perspective, implementation requires a hierarchical administrative structure that allows superiors to motivate and to control subordinates in the administrative bureaucracy and direct their activities towards the desired policy outcomes. This perspective also emphasizes the importance of building and maintaining political consensus regarding desired policy goals and performance within and among the government agencies and other organisations with responsibility for implementation, as well as with the external political system of government agencies, organisations and others with an interest in a policy's impact. The essence of this approach is the use of hierarchical planning and control to identify and eliminate, or at least contain, barriers to effective implementation. Such planning and control is seen as the best way to achieve specified policy goals.

Implementation as politics is another view of the implementation phase of the policy–making process. Policy and programme implementation, in this view, occurs primarily through the interaction, bargaining and negotiation among those actors with responsibility for the implementation as well as those affected, or potentially affected, by a policy or programme action. The policy goals and approaches that emerge during policy formulation provide the starting point for this bargaining and negotiating. Through this political interaction, policy goals and approaches are debated and redefined, as are implementation strategies. Planning and control of programme funding and other implementation activities are difficult, if not impossible, in this view. What actually emerges as policy during implementation is a function of the concerns and relative political power of the different parties — government agencies, political interest groups, community organisations and other groups — with an interest in a public policy and its implementation.

A fourth perspective on implementation recognises that the implementation process encompasses several sets of similar factors that individually or jointly foster or inhibit effective policy and programme implementation and thus the achievement of desired policy performance. Some factors are statutory in nature. For example, administrative regulations and standard operating procedures must be specified that will effectively transform policy objectives into actual policy achievements. If such regula-

33

tions and operating procedures are not clearly defined and feasible, they will hinder the achievement of desired policy outcomes. Implementation is also affected by non-statutory factors, external to the policy–making process. Social, economic and techno-logical conditions, for example, affect public perceptions of policy problems. If these conditions are such that they help maintain and enhance public support for dealing with a problem, the likelihood of effective implementation is increased. Such public support weighs against the arguments of opposing interests. The nature of the policy problem itself also affects the likelihood of effective policy implementation. Successful implementation becomes less certain the greater the individual and collective be-havioural changes required by a policy initiative. From this fourth perspective, then, effective implementation depends upon a composite of statutory structures, non-statutory forces and problem tractability.

Implications for Institutional Partnerships

The policy implementation process is the critical link between formulating policy goals and strategies and achieving desired outcomes. Each of the four perspectives on implementation emphasize different attributes of this process. Taken together, these perspectives provide an overall characterisation of this phase of the policy–making process. This characterisation suggests at least three important broad realities that should be reflected in the organisation and operation of institutional partnerships used for implementing public policies and programmes for rural areas. These three realities reflect the notion of the policy implementation process as an administrative process, a political process and a process involving a substantial degree of uncertainty.

The first broad reality is that implementation is, as it tends to be viewed tradition-ally, an administrative process. As such, it requires attention to planning, resource adequacy and allocation, co–operation and co–ordination among the agencies and organisations responsible for implementation, understandable and feasible operating rules and procedures, adequate managerial capacity and other conditions for effective administration.

Planning and implementation of programmes in the Netherlands initiated under the Rural Redevelopment Act requires the involvement of numerous partners representing all levels of government, the private sector, producer associations and community groups. The effective functioning of this partnership arrange-ment requires broad–based political support for the rural development programmes initiated, close working relationships among the partners and ade-quate financial support. The Rural Redevelopment Act was put into effect in 1979 and foresees a long–term partnership including numerous institutions co–operating on precise and legally–binding procedures. This multiple arrange-ment is regarded as the most effective means to address the problems of struc-tural unemployment and general economic stagnation in the East Groningen area and peat district of Groningen and Drenthe.

Another broad reality is that, while implementation is an administrative process, it is also fundamentally a political process. It involves much more than government bureaucrats putting the intent of public policies into effect. Implementation involves a continuation of the debate, bargaining and negotiating about basic societal values, policy goals and strategies, and programme priorities initiated during the formulation phase of the policy–making process.

A third reality is that the implementation process tends to be characterised by a substantial degree of uncertainty. It is not a straightforward, automatic process with well–defined and clearly articulated parameters. As a consequence, implementation tends to be an adaptive, evolutionary as opposed to a rational pre–programmed, step–by–step process. For example, policy goals, programme strategies and resource commitments developed during the formulation phase of the policy–making process set the initial parameters and conditions for policy implementation. Often, however, experience demonstrates that the policy problem was not well understood. In addition, public policies may have multiple, ill–defined goals, requiring implementors to not only select those goals they can reasonably expect to address in an effective fashion, but also to specify those goals more clearly. Suggested programme strategies may not always reflect current managerial and technological capacities of the agencies with responsibility for implementation. Initial resource commitments may well be inadequate to effectively carry out suggested programme initiatives. Also, social, economic and technological conditions may change over time, affecting the nature of the policy problem and political support for addressing it in a concerted fashion.

These and other such developments must be dealt with during the implementation process. It is not possible to anticipate and plan for all of these developments; consequently, implementation is characterised by substantial uncertainty. While rational, programmed, step–by–step implementation strategies can help anticipate and provide an overall operational structure for addressing some of these developments, they also tend to limit the implementing organisation's ability to respond flexibly and creatively to changing circumstances. Adaptive implementation, on the other hand, deals with the uncertainties of policy implementation by adjusting initial goals, programme strategies, operating procedures and other factors as circumstances change.

Chapter V

ORGANISING AND OPERATING
RURAL DEVELOPMENT PARTNERSHIPS

Most OECD Member countries have had considerable experience in using various types of institutional partnerships for implementing public policies and programmes for rural areas. Member country experience indicates clearly that several conditions play an important role in setting the stage for the formation of a partnership and its eventual success. The following three conditions, while not an exhaustive listing, appear particularly important. First, there must be a clear sense that an important problem situation exists and that some form of public or public–private partnership arrangement is a reasonable strategy for addressing the situation. Second, while the partnership arrangement must offer hope for resolving the problem situation, it also must offer an opportunity for each partner to benefit in some way. Benefits may occur in many forms, including increased contact with policymakers, greater visibility and a larger role in the policy formulation and implementation processes, better information on and understanding of rural conditions and problems, and economic and other benefits accruing to individual partners from policies and programmes initiated and implemented through the partnership. Third, each partner must have the motivation and commitment to make the partnership work. Partners must have the patience and perseverance to work at implementing rural policies and programmes over the long run, each partner working through difficult times as well as good times.

Beyond these basic conditions that set the stage for forming rural development partnerships, the effective functioning of these partnerships depend on numerous organisational, managerial and political factors. These factors are inherent to all types and forms of institutional partnerships as organisational entities operating within the context of the policy implementation process. They can be grouped in the following categories: political feasibility, organisation, managerial capacity, communication and co–ordination.

Political Feasibility

Member country experience in using institutional partnerships for implementing rural policies indicates that the politics of partnership implementation are as important as the politics of policy formulation. Political feasibility is a crucial issue in both the organisation and operation of institutional partnerships.

It is important to analyse the political feasibility of partnership implementation from both an internal and an external perspective when assessing the potential of institutional partnerships for rural policy implementation. Sound *a priori* analysis of political feasibility, analysis undertaken before becoming embroiled in the details of organising and operating a partnership arrangement, will help bridge the gap between partnership ideas that seem desirable and those that are possible. *A priori* political feasibility analysis will help limit wasteful investment of political, financial and other scarce resources in institutional partnership strategies which are likely to be ineffective or fail because of their political liabilities.

When analysing the political feasibility of a policy or implementation strategy, several categories of information are particularly useful to consider. These categories include: actors; values, beliefs, and motivations of actors; actors' resources; and points of political consensus and conflict among actors. Actors include all parties likely to be affected by and interested in partnership activities. An actor can be a government department or agency, a regional or communal government, a business or an industry, a professional association, a voluntary community organisation, a co-operative, a non-profit organisation, or an individual.

The Rural Policy Advisory Committee in Sweden was created in 1977 with the purpose of improving economic and social conditions in rural Sweden. The Advisory Committee is a partnership among representatives of central and county government, political parties, and several interest groups concerned with rural issues. The Advisory Committee has played a leading catalyst role in the formulation of rural policy. Unlike the numerous other government agencies and organisations concerned with rural issues which represent primarily sectorial or special interests, the Rural Policy Advisory Committee has responsibility for taking an integrated, global approach to rural issues and rural policy.

Analysis of who the actors are, their values, beliefs and motivations, and their resources in the context of a possible rural development partnership arrangement and its purpose will provide insights into probable points of political consensus and conflict. It will help delineate which actors will be supportive, which will not, and which resources will be used, and how, to effectuate support or opposition. It will elucidate the political feasibility of partnership implementation, and provide a basis for deciding whether to invest scarce resources into organising an institutional partnership strategegy.

Organisation

Organisation is an important factor in enhancing the effectiveness of any institutional partnership. Organisation involves establishing a structure to carry out those activities or functions necessary to achieve the goals and objectives of the partnership. In establishing this structure, functions are grouped into general categories and authority and responsibility are assigned to individuals and groups to carry out those functions. In the context of most organisations, these general categories of functions include planning, organising, staffing, directing, and controlling.

In addition to establishing the structure and specifying the general functions of a partnership for rural development, experience in many OECD Member countries indicates that several other factors are important in partnership organisation. These factors seem to stand out and are often mentioned in the context of Member country experience:

— an appropriate and clearly–defined constitutional and legal framework for undertaking partnership arrangements;
— major goals and objectives for partnership activities which are clearly defined, well understood, and mutually accepted by all partners;
— clearly–defined roles and responsibilities for all participating partners; and
— well–defined and mutually agreed–upon procedures for cost– and risk–sharing.

For most partnerships grounded in other than loosely–held political agreements, the constitutional and legal framework for undertaking partnership activities is important. It defines the societal roles and responsibilities of a partnership by specifying what the partnership is and does, and what it is not and does not do. It provides a recognised, accepted and legally legitimate basis for taking decisions, acquiring and allocating resources, and carrying out those programme activities and initiatives necessary to achieve partnership goals. Fundamentally, the constitutional and legal framework details the purpose of a partnership and identifies the legal basis and parameters of its actions for partners and nonpartners alike, thus clarifying and defining a legitimate role for the partnership in society. Lack of a clearly–defined constitutional and legal framework can cloud the perceived legal legitimacy of a partnership, undercutting its ability to operate effectively.

In 1983, the Finnish government initiated the Rural Occupations Experiment, designed to address the problem of employment generation in rural Finland. The experiment was a success, and it resulted in a permanent rural occupations programme. A core element of this programme is an institutional partnership involving central, provincial and communal governments that decentralises considerable decision–making authority to the provincial level. Provincial governments have key reponsibility for reviewing locally–initiated rural occupations projects and deciding which ones to subsidise. Through this decentralised intergovernmental partnership arrangement, Finland hopes to more effectively address the varying employment generation needs caused by the socio–economic diversity of its rural areas.

For partnerships to operate effectively, it is important that both the leadership and supporting roles and responsibilities of each partner be clearly defined and articulated. Furthermore, it is important that all partners understand and agree on these roles. Clearly–defined roles and responsibilities not only provide direction and focus to the contributions of individual partners, they also detail the boundaries of one partner's responsibilities relative to another's. Detailing these boundaries is important because it highlights the interdependence among partners' roles and responsibilities, thus helping to define situations or activities requiring close co–operation and co–ordination.

In some Member countries, intergovernmental partnerships designed to address the needs of rural areas often define planning and finance responsibilities for national, regional and local government partners. Clearly, for such partnerships to implement programmes effectively, each partner must understand its planning or finance roles and responsibilities as it relates to the like roles of other partners. Clear definition of these roles and responsibilities will delineate the interdependence of the partners in planning and finance and indicate the scope and nature of the co–operation and co–ordination required among them. When all partners understand and agree on their relative roles and responsibilities, misunderstanding, conflict and duplication of effort are reduced, allowing the partnership to more efficiently and effectively implement its programmes.

A fourth important factor in partnership organisation is clearly–defined and mutually agreed–upon procedures for cost and risk sharing. From a societal perspective, one of the advantages of institutional partnership arrangements is that they provide a mechanism for marshalling and melding the financial, personnel, managerial, political and other resources of multiple partners and committing those resources to resolving important economic, environmental and societal problems in rural areas. From the perspective of individual partners, however, this process raises questions about the distribution of financial and other resource commitments and political risks associated with policy and programme implementation among the partners.

For most actors to be willing to participate as partners and to make a long–term commitment to partnership goals, the bounds of each potential partner's exposure to the costs and risks must be specified, understood and accepted as reasonable. Without clearly–defined agreements and procedures for cost– and risk–sharing, potential partners are not as likely to make the transition from actor to partner. If they do enter into a partnership arrangement under these circumstances, they are likely to limit their involvement in ways designed to protect their financial and political interests, which in turn will likely limit the effectiveness of the partnership as a vehicle for policy implementation.

Managerial Capacity

Organisational and management capacity is crucial to the success of any rural development partnership. This concern, while an obvious consideration, surfaces continually in the experiences of most Member countries in using partnership arrangements, indicating the pervasiveness of the problem and its importance. Recent discussions on intercommunal or intergovernmental partnerships at the local government level in France drew attention to the fact that the effectiveness of these partnerships might be somewhat limited by the management capacity of elected local government officials. Equally, state and regional government partnerships in France might sometimes lack capacity and initiative and therefore limit partnership effectiveness. Inadequate managerial capacity for the smooth operation of the planning contract partnership for rural development has been cited as an obstacle in the Amvrakikos Gulf Partnership in Greece.

The organisational capacity of partnerships depends on its ability to:

— Anticipate and influence change;
— Make informed, intelligent decisions about policy;
— Develop programmes to implement policy;

- Attract and absorb resources;
- Manage resources; and
- Evaluate current activities to guide future action.

In 1987, as part of its programme for balanced and equitable development of the rural environment, the Walloon Regional Executive (Belgium) requested the Fondation Rurale de Wallonie (FRW) to run an experimental rural development initiative grounded in institutional partnerships. The FRW's standing concern is to rally agents of rural development. With offices in 6 areas of Wallonia, growing specialisation among local staff, and its marketing unit and operations service, this private–law foundation acts as a catalyst for the efforts of local councils, government services and private–sector agents to foster development in rural areas. It provides help with the development of rural enterprises, the diversification of agricultural industries, the establishment of rural tourism and infrastructure, through partnerships. Its experience makes it a prime partner for the Walloon authorities in formulating rural policy.

Furthermore, for rural development partnerships to be operated effectively, they must be grounded in adequate authority and have access to financial resources and leadership. Other important factors that affect the capacity of partnerships to effectively implement rural policies and programmes include staff, information and mechanisms to monitor and assess partnership functioning and policy and programme performance.

To have the capacity to function effectively, institutional partnerships for rural policy implementation must be able to adapt to social and economic change, make informed decisions, implement policies and programmes, attract and manage financial and other resources, and monitor and evaluate programme performance as a guide to future action. To accomplish these tasks effectively, partnerships require adequate authority, financial resources and leadership.

The new rural policy in Austria is based on a series of partnerships between federal and regional government and between the public and private sectors. "Endogenous renewal" and "self–reliant development" are the fundamental principles underlying the new rural policy. The Austrian government is looking to its new rural development policy as a means to alleviate problems of economic decline and unemployment in Eastern Austria. Numerous policies and programmes have been initiated in the Waldviertel, a region in northeast Austria. A complex set of operational mechanisms was put in place, each stipulating resources, roles and responsibilities of the actors concerned. The legal basis for the arrangement has been worked out in detail in order to strengthen the authority of the various programmes. Care has been taken to ensure that the overall organisational framework, despite its complexity, remains comprehensible.

The need to strengthen these requirements will vary among different partnership arrangements. This need will also vary among partners participating in a particular partnership. However, in organising and operating partnerships for rural policy implementation, OECD Member country experience shows that organisational and managerial capacity in its various dimensions is a crucial issue that must be addressed if partnerships are to succeed. The characteristics and requirements for organisational and managerial capacity noted in this section may suggest possible policy and programme opportunities for strengthening the capacity of various partners and partnership arrangements. In the context of intercommunal partnerships in France, for example, it has been suggested that central government should play a strong role in providing management training adapted to the needs of elected local government officials.

Communication

Effective communication of rural policy goals and implementation procedures is a prerequisite for effective policy implementation. An important element in organising and operating rural development partnerships is the establishment of a communication system and procedures that allow information to be transmitted with clarity and consistency. Information concerning policy goals and procedures for programme implementation may be transmitted only partially or not at all because an adequate communication system has not been put into place, or if it has, it has not been effectively managed. For rural development partnerships to be successful in implementing policies and programmes for rural areas, care must be taken to ensure that an adequate system is established for communicating policy and programme information among all partners and those involved in day–to–day implementation tasks.

The Regional Secretaries in Switzerland run the administrative side of their regions, co–ordinate local policy and assist in the implementation of development programmes. Though without policy–making power, the Regional Secretaries occupy a key position at the intersection of social, political and institutional relations. Their key role as a co–ordinator, counsellor and promoter leads them to:

— maintain contacts with economic interests concerned with rural development;
— encourage involvement in rural development schemes; and
— support and advise on initiatives that foster rural development.

Through their activities they help develop a partnership among the agents of rural development: elected officeholders, local communities and entrepreneurs.

For implementation to proceed smoothly, not only must information be transmitted, but it must be transmitted with clarity. Implementors must understand the policy and programme goals to be achieved and the implementation rocedures to be followed. Vaguely–defined goals and procedures can hinder implementation. Vagueness increases the probability that implementors will misinterpret policymakers' intent with respect to what purposes are to be achieved, what people and places are to be affected by a policy, and what procedures are to be used in carrying out a policy. The policy goal, for example, of improving rural community water systems is vague. The word "improving" is unclear. It does not provide implementors much guidance regarding what, specifically, is to be achieved. Vaguely defined policy goals, programme standards and implementation procedures are open to interpretation, and thus can foster debate among multiple, conflicting political interests both within the implementing bureaucracy and external to it, which serves to hinder the implementation process.

While vagueness can be problematical for implementation, so can too much specificity. Rural policy goals, programme standards and implementation procedures that are too specific and detailed can hinder implementation by making it difficult to adapt programmes to the diverse needs of different rural areas. Specificity and clarity, however, are not necessarily synonymous. The intent of public policies, the definition of target groups and standards for involving them in programmes, appropriate operating procedures and other factors important in policy implementation can be communicated clearly with being overly specific or detailed.

Consistency is another element of communication important for effective implementation. Inconsistencies in communication of policy and programme information can result from several factors. For example, multiple policy goals may be communicated that are inconsistent. Improving environmental quality and increased rural industrialisation may be inconsistent goals. When different levels of government and several agencies at the same governmental level are actively involved in implementation, it is often the case that multiple, sometimes inconsistent policy statements and procedural directions may arise. Inconsistencies may also arise because the demands of numerous, conflicting political interests have been accommodated in both the policy formulation and implementation processes. Inconsistency in communicating about policy goals and procedures for achieving these goals during implementation can create conflict and cause confusion among those responsible for implementation, thus limiting the effectiveness of that process.

Co-ordination

Co-ordination is one of the key factors in determining whether public policies and programmes are successfully implemented. It is an important aspect of organising and operating institutional partnerships for rural policy implementation. Partnership arrangements may include different agencies or departments from the same level of government, different levels of government, and partners from the private as well as the public sector. These partners must work jointly to marshall and to direct available resources in carrying out policy and programme actions. Member country experience suggests that efficient and effective operation of institutional partnerships for implementing rural policy depends upon the degree of success achieved in co-ordination.

Co-ordination involves deliberate, joint and often formalized relations among individuals, groups and organisations for achieving shared goals. It is both a structure and a process of concerted decision-making or action wherein two or more parties work jointly to achieve some collective purpose. Viewed as structure, co-ordination involves specifying the nature of working relationships, and thus the structure of relative power and autonomy, among participants. Viewed as process, co-ordination is concerned with mechanisms and processes for joint decision-making.

43

In Italy, the Permanent Conference for Planning for the Veneto province operates within the policy framework of the Mountain Project. The Conference involves a partnership between communal and regional government administrations for the purpose of implementing a global, territorial policy. The Conference consists of each of the presidents and mayors from the mountain communities in Veneto and the presidents of the mountain provinces of Belluro, Treviso, Vicenza and Verona and the mayors of three designated mountain communities. It is headed by the President of the Regional Council or by a delegated regional Councillor. The Conference is responsible for direction, control, follow–up and co–ordination of planning in the Venetian mountain areas.

The purpose of the Mountain Project is to co–ordinate planning and implementation of rural policies and programmes for mountainous areas in the province of Veneto. The specific objectives of the Mountain Project are to promote the active involvement of mountain people in the regional planning process and to define objectives for public policies and programmes. The project encompasses the important sectors of regional intervention, and covers approximately one–third of the Venetian territory.

From a technical organisational and managerial perspective, co–ordination requires that the issues of autonomy, centralisation, specialised authority and responsibility be addressed. The autonomy issue deals with how programme administration responsibilities should be shared among partners in an institutional partnership arrangement. Should one partner take the primary lead in administering a programme, or should the responsibility be shared among the partners involved? The specialised authority issue focuses on the extent to which important decision–making and staff positions necessary for carrying out implementation tasks should be filled by technical subject–matter experts instead of generalists, by career bureaucrats instead of political appointees. Embedded in this issue is the question of the relative distribution of authority and power among the staff and line or operating units and among generalist politicians and technical experts within a partnership arrangement. The responsibility issue centres on the distribution of the workload and the resources associated with implementing a policy or programme among the partners involved. Another dimension of this issue centres on who controls the flow of work and the distribution of resources.

Establishing a structure and procedures for co–ordinating the resources and actions of multiple partners in a partnership arrangement involves complex decisions about allocating authority and power in the implementation process. Co–ordination is essentially a political process.

Chapter VI

CONCLUSIONS

Principal Findings

The experience reported in this study on institutional partnerships for rural development seems to indicate that most successful partnerships have been built up gradually in response to changing rural policy needs through the involvement of the public administration and a broad spectrum of public and private actors. They are the result of long processes of institutional evolution rather than of single political decisions or *a priori* considerations of administrative or societal design.

Partnerships have originally been developed under very different constitutional, political and administrative systems, but, over time, show a tendency to converge in form and function, as specific rural policy necessities gain precedence over traditional administrative parameters in setting standards for successful arrangements.

The study has shown that partnerships have a record of comparative advantage in their capacity to effectively co-ordinate public and private interests, human and financial resources, legal and administrative bases and political authority to pursue agreed-upon objectives and to share risks and responsibilities.

In many countries, they have been shown to be particularly suitable for facilitating the policy-making process. Partnerships have proven to be mechanisms capable of fostering co-operation among various sectoral departments, articulating the functional complementarity of different levels of government, and to associate and provide political legitimacy to a wide range of private economic and social interests.

Moreover, partnerships are flexible arrangements, allowing for many organisational and administrative models and modalities which can, in comparison with traditional arrangements of public administration, be more easily renegotiated and adapted more rapidly to accomodate the evolving development opportunities in the wide variety of rural situations.

Finally, the reported experience shows that, in order to be effective, partnerships depend on a number of essential political, managerial and administrative prerequisites. The following paragraphs summarise these essential prerequisites in the field of political feasibility, organisation, managerial capacity, communication and co-ordination.

An Institutional Response to Rural Policy Needs

Large-scale structural changes in the rural economy and society, the recognition of the importance of rural areas for the maintenance of a sound biosphere and sometimes far—reaching reforms in public administrative systems have posed fundamental challenges for rural policy—making in many OECD Member countries. These challenges include gaining a better understanding of the interrelatedness of current socio-economic, environmental and political trends and issues in rural areas, which, much more than in the past, are shaped by a direct interaction among local, national and international developments.

One of the most striking issues in Member countries' efforts to accomodate these structural changes in rural areas is the trend towards comprehensive, integrated policies. Such global approaches seem more often to have evolved out of a gradual recognition of a series of sectoral interdependencies than to be the result of a grand design.

Intimately related to this gradual process of policy reorientation is the search in most Member countries for more effective institutional arrangements for rural policy formulation and implementation. A wide variety of mechanisms has been put in place to accommodate the need for a more global, and often territorial, approach to rural policy, which at the same time accounts for rural diversity, decentralised governmental authority and the trend towards increased private sector involvement in the pursuit of public rural policies.

While the diversity of political, administrative and constitutional systems in Member countries certainly explains the differences in form, scale, legal basis and institutional origin of these mechanisms, there is evidence that the nature of the rural policy issues to be addressed in all Member countries gradually has led to the establishment of rather comparable institutional arrangements, of which partnerships are the most common.

Forms Adaptable to Scale and Purpose

Institutional partnerships take many forms, are used for many purposes, and often involve complex legal, political, organisational and financial interrelationships among partners. The essence of any partnership, however, is an orchestration of policy and execution, based on shared objectives and priorities. The types and characteristics of institutional partnerships are numerous and vary with their purpose and scale, and often evolve over time. While it is not the objective here to detail a definitive general typology of institutional partnerships, the following features are important:

— Institutional partnerships may be grounded in formal, legally binding contractual arrangements, or they may involve informal, natural working relationships based on loosely—held political agreements;
— Institutional partnerships may be public sector partnerships involving departments and agencies at the same or different levels of government;
— Institutional partnerships may be public—private sector partnerships involving co—operation among departments and agencies at various levels of government and private sector partners, including non—profit organisations, professional associations, neighbourhood associations and community voluntary organisations as well as business;
— Institutional partnerships may be used for rural policy implementation within a broad rural policy domain (e.g. rural public service development), or for specific programmes (e.g. job training for dislocated and disadvantaged workers)·

— Institutional partnerships develop and evolve over time, with respect to the structure, function, and operation of the partnership and its domain of policy concern. Many partnership arrangements have passed through stages in their evolution where, due to changes in policy needs, they lost some of their original effectiveness and had to be adapted and/or renegotiated;
— Institutional partnerships can also vary according to their organisational and geographic scale. Some partnerships are very large in terms of their organisational and geographic reach, while others involve relatively small–scale organisations focused on a limited geographic area.

An Effective Instrument for Rural Policy

Partnerships now seem to be regarded as relatively effective instruments for capitalising on emerging opportunities and for addressing persisting or new problems in rural areas, since they bring together views and capacities of many sectoral departments, different levels of government and a wide spectrum of private economic and social interests.

This is particularly true in the crucial business of policy implementation. In many countries, the ultimate viability of comprehensive rural policy–making is seen to depend on the capacities of a considerable number of heterogeneous institutions to work out together durable forms of co–operation that go well beyond mutual consultations and negotiated goal–setting, but which also provide for the actual pooling of resources and sharing of risks and responsibilities during the implementation phase.

From a policy perspective, institutional partnerships:

i) Can be mechanisms for merging the perspectives, experiences and resources of multiple institutional and individual actors necessarily involved in an integrated, territorial approach to rural policy;

ii) If properly structured, are capable of providing the flexibility necessary to identify and to respond more efficiently and effectively to the diverse local socio–economic and political circumstances of rural areas;

iii) Can help organise and enhance complementarity of rural development programme purpose and action vertically among levels of government and horizontally across governmental units at the same level, thus focusing energies and resources in a more concerted fashion on critical problems; and

iv) Can provide a means to organise and to capitalise on the advantages of the pragmatic public and private sector co–operation emerging in rural areas.

From a political economy perspective, many public and private sector actors may well see participation in partnership arrangements as a means to further their own operational and political interests.

Prerequisites for Effectiveness

OECD Member country experience indicates that the effective functioning of institutional partnerships for rural policy implementation depends on several organisational, managerial and political prerequisites. These factors are inherent in all types and forms of institutional partnerships as organisational entities operating within the context of the policy implementation process. These important factors may be interpreted as prerequisites as well as limits, in their absence, to effective functioning of institutional partnerships. They can be grouped in the following general categories: political feasibility, organisation, mangerial capacity, communication, and co-ordination. Member country experience indicates that the following specific factors, while not necessarily an exhaustive listing, are important in organising and operating institutional partnerships for rural policy implementation.

Political Feasibility

Partnership goals, representation, organisational structure, and operating procedures must be politically feasible from the perspective of both those internal and those external to the partnership.

Organisation

i) An organisational system and structure must be established to carry out the general planning, organising, funding, staffing, directing and controlling functions necessary for the partnership to achieve its goals and objectives.
ii) The constitutional and legal framework for undertaking partnership agreements must be clearly specified.
iii) Major goals and objectives for partnership activities must be clearly defined, well understood, and shared by all partners.
iv) Procedures for sharing the costs and risks associated with partnership activities must be well-defined and agreed upon by all partners.

Managerial Capacity

i) Adequate authority (formal or legal and informal), access to financial resources, and leadership, all prime determinants of organisational and managerial capacity, are necessary for partnership arrangements to function effectively.
ii) The organisational and managerial capacity of institutional partnerships is also dependent upon the availability of well-trained staff, adequate and appropriate information on rural policy performance and mechanisms for monitoring and evaluating policy performance and partnership functioning.

Communication

A communication system must be established that allows information to be transmitted with clarity and consistency, both to partners and those working within the partnership organisation and to those parties external to the partnership.

Co-ordination

A structure and a process for co-ordinating the resources and actions of the multiple partners involved in a partnership arrangement must be established if rural policies and programmes are to be effectively implemented.

Part II

PARTNERSHIPS FOR RURAL DEVELOPMENT
IN SELECTED COUNTRIES

INTRODUCTION

Part I of the report is based on the contributions by the Member countries which have taken part in the OECD Activity on Rural Public Management. The country contributions have been summarised in Part II.

In order to allow a measure of comparability, the experience of each Member country is presented in a similar format. A short summary, at the head of each country contribution, indicates the partnership being analysed, its purpose and some of the main partners involved. Within each contribution, partnership arrangements are described in terms of their objectives, rationale and broad policy context, procedures, implementation and overall effectiveness.

The main purpose of Part II is to set out specific examples of institutional partnerships. These examples help to highlight the important aspects of partnership systems and their operation described in Part I. They also indicate the potential that partnership systems may hold for implementing development policies in rural areas.

AUSTRIA

SUMMARY

The new rural policy in Austria is based on a partnership between federal and regional government and between the public and private sectors. "Endogenous renewal" and "self–reliant development" are the fundamental principles underlying the new rural policy. These principles and numerous policies and programmes that stem from them have been initiated in the Waldviertel, a region in northeast Austria. The Austrian government is looking to its new rural development policy as a means to alleviate problems of economic decline and unemployment in Eastern Austria.

NEW RURAL DEVELOPMENT POLICY

Unequal regional economic development between Eastern and Western Austria has led the Austrian Government to question its traditional rural development policy. The Government has initiated a new rural policy based on the principles of "endogenous renewal" and "self–reliant development". Implementation of this new rural policy relies on partnerships between federal and regional government and between the public and private sectors. This summary describes Austria's new rural policy, its constitutional framework, some of the institutions and instruments for implementing it, and experience applying its underlying principles in the Waldviertel Region of northeast Austria.

The following features characterise the regional distribution of economic activity in Austria:

- In relation to the economic center of Western Europe, Austria lies on the eastern edge.
- Tendencies toward strong regional concentration are the result of structural changes in the agricultural sector, which has lost more than two–thirds of its labour force over the last decades.
- In Western Austria, structural change in agriculture did not result in loss of income or population due primarily to development of the tourist industry. In Eastern Austria, however, most peripheral rural areas experienced considerable population loss and far–above–average unemployment rates.

- Many of the firms which settled in the rural areas of Eastern Austria in the 1960s and early 1970s were unable to survive the economic crisis of the early and mid–1980s.
- Locational circumstances and the lack of an appropriate socio–economic climate impede the establishment of a diversified industrial structure in the old industrial regions of Eastern Austria, which have proved to be the main problem for rural policy.

These five factors have led to a decline in economic growth rates in Eastern Austria, and the gap between Eastern and Western Austria has grown wider in recent years.

The New Regional Policy

In view of the unequal economic development between Eastern and Western Austria, and as it has been recognised that traditional rural policy is no longer adequate, the new rural policy is oriented toward the principle of "endogenous renewal" and has the following features:

- Mobilisation of potential of the rural areas;
- Structural policy above job creation policy;
- Transfer of information above transfer of capital;
- Development of human capital above development of material capital;
- Promotion of co–operative activities above promotion of individual firms; and
- Decentralisation of rural development policy and programme planning and implementation.

Constitutional Framework

Austria is a federal state with three political levels: the federal government, nine regional or *Land* governments, and some 2 300 local governments. In Austria, rural policy is not only a matter of just one of these three levels of government; rather, it is a dimension of the constitutional powers of each level. This situation makes it imperative for the federal, regional and local governments to co–operate extensively on all rural development policy matters.

The opportunity to conclude agreements between the federal government and the *Lander* in the form of "state treaties" is an important constitutional tool for putting co–operative rural development programmes on a firm legal basis. State treaties have been increasingly used for this purpose since the beginning of the 1980s. The most important institution for co–ordinating rural development activities as envisaged under the concept of the co–operative federal state is the "Austrian Conference on Regional Planning" set up at the national level in 1971 as a permanent joint body of the federal, regional and local governments.

The constitutional framework for rural development policy in Austria is designed to promote national coherence and reduce regional disparities. These objectives can only be pursued if close co–operation of all parties concerned is possible. Therefore, it has been a tradition for governments in Austria to co–operate with the private sector. There are a variety of ways for such co–operation to occur, and in recent years the number of quangos has been increasing.

Institutions and Instruments of the Federal Government

The Austrian Association for Self–reliant Regional Development is an umbrella organisation of nine regional associations dealing with self–reliant regional development. The Association promotes and supports the exchange of experiences between projects and associations from the various rural areas, organises training courses, and provides regional consultants to disadvantaged rural areas. These consultants offer advice on innovative economic initiatives and fiscal matters. They attend to projects from conception until the projects become operative.

The Österreichische Studien und Beratungregesellschaft: Alternativ–und Sanierungskonzepte für Regionen und Betreibe (ÖSB) is a non–party, non–profit association. The ÖSB has approximately 400 members from self–administered and traditionally operated enterprises, universities and research establishments, the Chambers of Labour, trade unions and youth organisations as well as lawyers and tax consultants. It was set up in 1981 for the purpose of providing information, advice and training to self–administered enterprises and social job creation projects. The organisation's main tasks are the organisation of training courses for project staff members, the strengthening of co–operation and co–ordination among projects and the provision of advice on developing and operating self–administered enterprises or social projects through a team of six management consultants.

On the basis of an amendment to the Labour Market Promotion Act, the labour market authorities have been able since 1983 to provide incentives for setting up:

— Enterprises that create jobs for unemployed persons or workers threatened by unemployment, the staff of which must participate essentially and equally in enterprise operation; and
— Non–profit, self–help facilities which create jobs for unemployed persons or workers who are threatened by unemployment (social job–creating initiatives).

In addition to such project–related incentives, the labour market authorities also provide person–related incentives for the employment of jobless people.

THE WALDVIERTEL AREA — AN EXAMPLE

The Waldviertel lies in the northeast of Austria where the state of lower Austria borders on Czechoslovakia, and comprises four administrative districts with some 160 000 inhabitants. Recent rural development initiatives in this area illustrate the application of Austria's new rural development policy.

The Waldviertel Area

This area is a "weakly–developed problem area", characterised by the predominance of agriculture, peripheral areas with an economic potential far below the national average and substantial labour market problems. The industrialised part of the area suffers from structural weaknesses because its industry is dominated by small and medium–sized enterprises heavily dependent on externally–controlled subsidiaries. In recent years, conditions in the labour market have been characterised by decreasing job opportunities and high unemployment rates.

The Waldviertel Plan

The Waldviertel Plan is based on a study prepared by the Austrian Regional Planning Institute (ÖIR) in consultation with the competent federal ministries, the Office of the Lower Austrian Government, representatives from industry and the *Waldveriel* Regional Development Committee. In 1980 joint decisions were taken at the political level on the proposals made by the study.

Among the study proposals, the following are of particular importance:

- Promote settlement of industries and assist already existing industries to create additional jobs;
- Intensify technological, sales and management counselling services for existing companies in the Waldviertel;
- Establish spas and recreational centres as well as holiday villages in order to enhance development of the tourist industry;
- Create additional production and sales opportunities for the agricultural sector;
- Expand the communications system network in the area; and
- Improve and expand the rail network leading to major district towns in the Waldviertel.

These proposals have decisively and directly shaped several rural policy measures of the federal as well as the lower Austrian governments. It was possible to achieve agreement with the various federal ministries and the lower Austrian government that, subject to financial and legal constraints, these proposals — the Waldviertel Plan — would be a joint working basis for the federal and lower Austrian governments on rural policy matters.

Regional Development Policies

In implementing the Waldviertel Plan, a number of important rural development policies and programmes have been implemented by the federal and lower Austrian governments. The following initiatives are some of the more important ones:

- The Joint Special Promotion Scheme for Creating Jobs in industry, business, and tourism, initiated by the federal government and co–funded by the federal and lower Austrian governments;
- The Incentive Programme of the Federal Chancellery for Self–Reliant Rural Development, aimed at supporting innovative economic development projects likely to have a positive effect on disadvantaged regions; and
- Various federal and rural initiatives focusing on industrial job creation, financial incentives for industrial investment, tourism promotion, public transportation development, labour market promotion and agricultural modernisation.

Institutions and Instruments for Regional Development Policy

The Waldviertel Plan gave major impetus to the conclusion of the "State Treaty" between the federal and lower Austrian governments. The "State Treaty" comprises all rural development agreements between the federal and the lower governments.

In implementing the Waldviertel Plan, a "Regional Advisor of the Federal Government for the Waldviertel" was installed in 1980, with its headquarters in the Waldviertel. The Regional Advisor has rendered a decisive contribution to the development of health tourism. Moreover, the Advisor's support was essential for transforming local industry from a textile into a metal and electrical engineering industry.

Lower Austria, too, installed a "Regional Consultant for the Waldviertel", for counselling and advising on projects in the area. The Consultant's tasks include:

— Implementation of the new rural policy concepts;
— Development of the economy of the area, including agriculture and tourism;
— Support of local initiatives;
— Strengthening of regional awareness; and
— Public relations activities promoting the image of the Waldviertel.

In implementing these tasks, the Consultant is in permanent contact with the elected politicians of the Waldviertel, the professional associations, the administrative district authorities and mayors as well as the competent authorities of the *Land* government.

The Regional Managers of the *Land* Government and the Regional Planning Advisory Councils also play important roles in implementing rural development policy in the Waldviertel. The regional managers of the *Land* Government focus on development of tourism facilities, particularly holiday villages, and marketing of endogenous agricultural products. The Regional Planning Advisory Councils are lower Austria's major regional policy institutions. The Councils assist the local authorities and regional planning associations with regard to the regional planning activities of the *Land* government.

CONCLUSIONS

In summing up, the Waldviertel area may be described as a pilot area for co–operative efforts involving the federal and *Land* governments and public sector and private institutions dealing with rural development. In general, the Waldviertel experience shows that co–operation is sometimes difficult for the federal and *Land* governments, which both pursue rural development policies on account of the responsibilities entrusted to them within the framework of the federal constitution. Recently, however, it has been possible to intensify and improve intergovernmental co–operation in the context of specific rural development projects.

The Waldviertel experience to date shows that a rural policy of "endogenous renewal" and "self–reliant development of regions" makes it almost imperative to take "help for self–help strategies" out of the sphere of public administration. In the Waldviertel, both the federal and the lower Austrian governments show signs of leaving the decision on the allocation of funds solely to the political institutions (Federal Chancellery, competent federal ministry or *Land* government), while conferring the responsibilities for counselling, incentive administration and project management largely upon quangos or paragovernmental institutions. This experience seems to indicate that rural development policy co–operation between public and private sector organisations can be most effectively achieved in the context of concrete individual projects.

Summary of institutional partnership activities by the example of the Waldviertel region

Institution or Instrument	Partners / Type of co-operative activity	Subject of co-operation / Division of tasks	Legal basis	Notes
State Treaty Federal-Lower Austrian Governments	Federal-Land governments Framework agreement between two territorial corportate bodies of different levels	Framework agreement on joint promotion and investment projects	State treaty as provided under federal constitution	Agreement covers all of Lower Austria, expires after 5 years
Joint Special Promotion Scheme for the Creation of Jobs	Federal and Land governments/ Programme agreement between two territorial bodies of different levels	Joint funding of incentive scheme (50:50) Agreement on the modalities of granting incentives	State treaty is framework agreement, identical decisions of the federal and Land governments	Initially, Waldviertel region the only assisted area, later on inclusion of other problem areas as defined in the Austrian Regional Planning Concept
Incentive Programme for Self-Reliant Regional Development (see also ÖAR below)	Federal administration (Federal Chancellery) - ÖAR, Programme agreement between territorial authority and private organisation	Federal government: procurement of funds and decision on allocation ÖAR: counselling on granting of funds, project supervision management, assignment of regional advisers	Private-law contract between the Federal Chancellery and ÖAR	Assisted areas also in other problem regions as defined in the Austrian Regional Planning Concept
Niederösterreichische Grenzlandförderungsgesellschaft GmbH (NÖG)	Federal and Land governments. Joint institution of territorial authorities in the form of a corporation	Promotion of Lower Austrian border areas by means of land procurement, development investment, acquisition of interest in enterprises, management consulting	Economic law	Scope of activity: Waldviertel region and other administrative districts near the state border
Regional Advisor of the Federal Government for the Waldviertel	Federal administration (Federal Chancellery) - private person	Order to advise and supervise projects in the region, to co-ordinate activities between promoter and federal agencies, to carry out "regional PR activities", as well as to co-operate with the regional consultant of the Land government	Private law agreement	Regional advisors of the federal government were also assigned to other problem areas as defined in the Austrian Regional Planning Concept
Regional Advisor of the Land government for the Waldviertel	Land administration - private person	Order to advise and supervise projects in the region, to co-ordinate activities among promotors, local authorities, professional organisations and offices of the Land government, and to carry out "regional PR activities"	Private law contract	The institution of the Regional Advisor of the Land exists only for the Waldviertel

Summary of institutional partnership activities by the example of the Waldviertel region *(cont'd)*

Institution or Instrument	Partners Type of co-operative activity	Subject of co-operation Division of tasks	Legal basis	Notes
Regional Manager of the Land administration	Assignment of civil servants of the Land administration to specific projects in the region	Project-related management of selected activities	Civil servants of the Land administration	The institution of the regional manager exists only for the Waldviertel
Regional Planning Advisory Councils	Land government - local authorities - professional organisations Joint advisory body	Preparation of concepts for regional development measures, forum of regional interests in matters of regional policy	Regional Policy Act	Set up for all planning regions of the Land
ECO PLUA Industrial Settlement and Regionalisation in Lower Austria Comp. Ltd.	Land government - companies (of the Land administration), the Land administration being the sole stockholder of a private company	Acquisitions for industrial settlements, promotion consulting, project managmenet of (existing) industrial centres, granting of funds by the Land government	Economic law	Competent for all of Lower Austria
Austrian Association for Self-reliant Regional Development (ÖAR), cf. also Incentive Programme for Self-reliant Regional Development	Umbrella organisation of nine regional associations dealing with self-reliant regional development and the BAF	Practical application of the concept of self-reliant regional development, exchange of experience among regional associations and projects; financed by the federal government; training and advanced training of regional consultants	Law on the formation of associations	Regional associations in all of Austria; for the Waldviertel: Waldviertler Bildungs- und Wirtschafts-initiative (BWI)
Österreichische Studien- und Beratungsgesellschaft: Alternativ- und Sanierungskonzepte für Regionen und Betriebe (ÖSB)	Labour market authorities - ÖSB Programme agreement between territorial authorities (Federal Ministry of Labour and Social Affairs) and private organisation	Implementation of new concepts for overcoming and/or preventing unemployment with the help of self-administered enterprises and social job-creating projects. Training and advanced training of advisors, management of project supervision. Financing of industrial settlement advisors by the federal government	Private-law contract between the federal Ministry of Labour and Social Affairs and the ÖSB	Management consulting and project supervision throughout Austria

BELGIUM

WALLONIA

SUMMARY

The Walloon Regional Executive's determination to promote an integrated rural development policy, in other words, one that is comprehensive, co–ordinated and transsectoral, has led to a close partnership bringing together representatives of central and local government and of the private sector via the *Fondation Rurale de Wallonie*. The *Foundation* is governed by private law but acts in a capacity guaranteed by government decree to provide consultancy services and logistical back–up to those involved in rural development, whether as regards equipment and infrastructure for local authorities, economic development of rural enterprises or diversification of agricultural activities. The *Foundation* is an important partner to government and other rural development actors because of its grassroots contacts, experience and the range of skills of its staff and collaborators.

THE ROLE OF THE *FONDATION RURALE DE WALLONIE* IN RURAL REVITALISATION POLICY

Wallonia (the French–speaking region of Belgium) covers the southern half of the country and has a population of 3.3 million, one–third of whom live in rural areas. In a context of demographic decline, at a time when agriculture is being restructured, the Walloon authorities have embarked upon a rural development policy centred around the notion of rural revitalisation. By its very nature, this policy implies establishing a range of multiple institutional partnership mechanisms, largely with the help of the *Fondation Rurale de Wallonie* (FRW). This summary, after a brief description of the *Foundation's* role in the rural revitalisation policy, reviews some examples of institutional partnerships that have been set up with its help.

According to the regionalisation laws of August 1980, Wallonia's economic development, and the quality of its environment and rural life is the responsibility of the

Walloon Region. In this context, the Region has initiated a dynamic rural development policy, centred around the theme of rural revitalisation, and called for its implementation through institutional partnerships. The Walloon Regional Executive has turned over the organisation of these experimental partnerships to the *Fondation Rurale de Wallonie*.

Rural Revitalisation Policy in Wallonia

The strong point of the rural revitalisation policy in the Walloon Region, and its originality, lie in its comprehensive approach. From the start, the Region sought to plan development in an integrated manner, i.e. to frame a comprehensive, co-ordinated and transsectoral policy. The Walloon Regional Executive made it quite clear in the order it adopted on 4th June 1987 that rural revitalisation "must consist of a coherent set of planning and development operations, undertaken in a rural area by local communal authorities and effectively mobilising its inhabitants, with a view to raising the standard of living of the population as a whole in economic, social and cultural respects".

In order to attain this objective, the Walloon authorities prefer endogenous development initiatives. The aim is to enable rural areas to take their own development in hand with the aid of different public or private sector partners. The Region takes part by funding projects concerned as much with improving communications as with promoting local economic activities. Various institutions act as intermediaries, providing a driving force for the implementation of this rural development policy. As well as being the point of liaison between the authorities and the population, they advise local authorities and involve other partners (e.g. the private sector, labour and management, research institutions, etc.) in the rural development process.

The Fondation Rurale de Wallonie

Recognising that a comprehensive policy for rural development was an original approach, the Walloon Regional Executive decided to entrust its implementation, on an experimental basis, to the *Fondation Rurale de Wallonie*.

The assignment of the *Foundation,* set up in 1975, is to promote rural development by mobilising all rural actors and promoting synergies among initiatives. The relationship between the Walloon Regional Executive and the FRW is by its very nature a public/private relationship, since the *Foundation,* like its counterparts in the United Kingdom or the United States, is a public–interest establishment which, in Belgium, is governed by private law.

The *Foundation* has a revolving fund financed by income from its capital (some US$130 000); its activities are subsidised by public authorities at central, regional and European levels. Managed by a board of directors, its accounts and the manner in which it uses the funds made available to it are subject to government control.

The *Foundation* makes its know–how available to local government (the "communes"), to the Walloon Regional Executive and to decisionmakers in the private sector. It provides technical and operational back–up in training and marketing to rural development actors. The *Foundation* operates through its field teams (working from area offices) and its consultants with scientific skills.

In the context of the Walloon Region's policy of balanced and equitable rural development, particularly through area–specific measures, the Walloon Regional Executive in November 1987 mandated the FRW to:

— Assist in the design of the Region's rural policy, especially as regards regional schemes *(Programme de Développement Régional, Plan de Rajeunissement de la Wallonie);*
— Assist in the design and implementation of legal and regulatory texts relating to rural revitalisation in terms of overall development promoting employment and the economy;
— Advise and assist municipalities that want to undertake a Rural Revitalisation programme, in particular by supplying leadership and inspiration to the working groups that are needed to prepare strategic plans;
— Provide back–up for municipalities engaged in the process of rural revitalisation, e.g. providing them with well–organised teams with the requisite skills. These teams are to help implement the development projects for which the municipalities have already signed agreements, and to assist in obtaining other agreements needed to realise municipal development objectives.

THE VARIOUS PARTNERSHIPS SET UP THROUGH THE FRW

As regards economic development, the FRW, together with the rural economy centre, the intercommunales and the sector committees concerned, contributes to the drafting of the non–agricultural chapters of the integrated plan for the development of South–Eastern Belgium. At the local and sub–regional levels, the *Foundation* is first of all a catalyst in associating the public and private sectors. Moreover, the *Foundation* has an important role of its own to play in the various kinds of institutional partnerships established.

The Institutional Partnership between the FRW and the Walloon Authorities

In the terms of the order of 4th June 1987, rural revitalisation policy involves the Council of the Commune:
— Deciding to pursue rural revitalisation objectives;
— Setting up machinery for consultation and participation by the public; and
— Establishing, jointly with the Local Revitalisation Commission and ad hoc working groups, a master plan and a multiannual and multisectoral programme, and prepares the various agreements needed.

The Council, by applying to the Minister responsible for the revitalisation of rural areas, can call on the FRW for help in the form of guidance from its staff, documentation and advice.

The Walloon Regional Executive considered, in establishing links with the *Foundation,* that the latter had been promoting ever since its inception a comprehensive development of rural areas by putting into practice at the grassroots the know–how and experience gained through its theoretical studies. The government of the Walloon Region recognised the worth of the knowledge amassed and enhanced by the FRW, and the fact that in serving rural development the *Foundation* uses the businesslike methods of the private sector. The public/private sector relationship thus entered into was first established through a three–year contract, subsequently through an annual subsidy, and in the end through a framework agreement. The resources provided the FRW by the Walloon Region do not, however, entirely cover all the *Foundation's* requirements or pay for all the activities it undertakes.

Alongside these arrangements, the rural revitalisation laid down by the Walloon Regional Executive ultimately provides for the approval by the appropriate ministers of the programme endorsed by the relevant section of the Regional Physical Planning Commission. This means that the government can ensure the consistency of sectoral policies, over which the FRW and its area offices are able to exert increasing influence.

The Establishment of a Multiple Partnership through the FRW

The FRW's primary assignment is to assist local administrations in fields as diverse as the expansion of rural tourism, the promotion of innovation in rural areas and the training of rural development experts. However, and equally importantly, it also forms partnerships with rural businesses, farmers and physical planners.

The *Foundation* also links dynamic and innovative firms and university research institutes in a variety of fields, such as management of the environment. With the help of the FRW's agronomists and development experts such firms can expand, widely diffuse the results of their work and take advantage of public sector programmes to support innovation. One example of this role was the assistance the *Foundation* was able to give to the Ménart company at Montroeul–au–Bois, a firm specialising in management of the environment and anxious to diversify its activities.

The *Foundation* establishes partnerships with farmers, also, placing its experience at their disposal to help them to diversify. In 1984, for instance, the Promagri group was set up, bringing together all the associations and organisations concerned with agricultural development in the Brabant Region. The aim was to diversify agricultural activity and to create a sector processing agricultural products. The FRW helped the group when it was launched, providing legal advice and logistical back–up, and continues to be a driving force behind the group even though its prospects now are extremely encouraging. For two years the FRW seconded one of its agronomists, part–time, to the Promagri group which, like the Promagri Diffusion company set up in 1987 to handle marketing for the group, still receives a great deal of assistance from the Foundation.

A whole range of elements — the training and experience of the FRW's development experts (many of whom are agronomists), their strong grassroots connections, their knowledge of local affairs, their ongoing concern with the region's natural and architectural heritage, the activities of the architectural assistance unit, the creation of many local committees concerned with environmental questions — has contributed to partnerships which have led, among other things, to:

— The collection of information dossiers on rural physical planning, associated outside experts, scientific advisers from the FRW, including officials from technical government services, architects, Ministry of Public Works officials, etc.;
— An inventory of the region's architectural assets, compiled in collaboration with the *Administration du patrimoine de la Communauté française*;
— Co–operation in formulating a development policy for national parks in the Region;

— A study of the architectural heritage of the Tournaisis area, carried out jointly by schools of architecture, an intercommunal body and the Tournai Maison de la Culture;

— The setting–up of nursery gardens run by the communes and the rehabilitation or creation of public parks and squares.

Thus the role of the FRW is in line with the Walloon authorities' desire not to encourage co–operation limited to a single or only a few institutions, which might generate "monopolistic practices". The pattern of partnership set by the *Foundation* calls for a convergence of views among the partners as regards policy objectives and programmes; it also involves the sharing of responsibilities, resources and risks over a given period. Moreover, as can be seen from the examples cited above, the partnerships are more of a relational than an institutional nature, and should be flexible enough to adapt as and when required to conditions in the field and to the pace at which action proceeds.

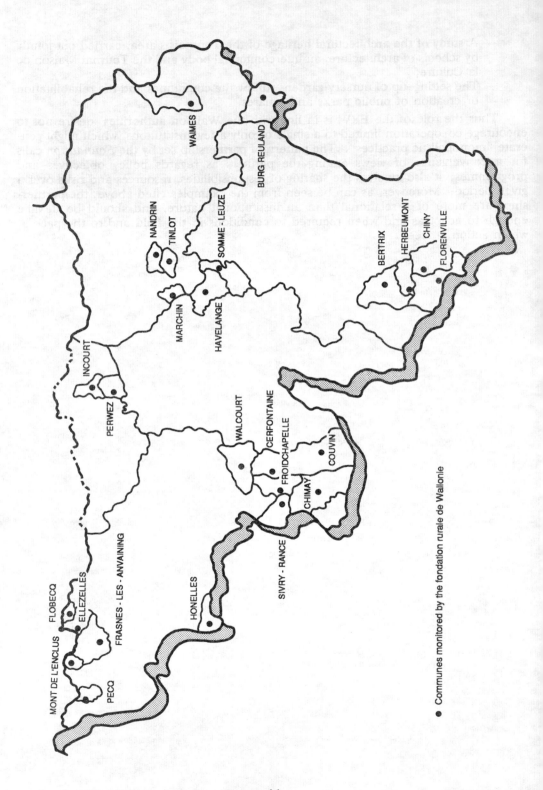

- Communes monitored by the fondation rurale de Wallonie

WAIMES
BURG REULAND
NANDRIN
TINLOT
SOMME - LEUZE
BERTRIX
HERBEUMONT
CHINY
FLORENVILLE
MARCHIN
HAVELANGE
INCOURT
PERWEZ
WALCOURT
CERFONTAINE
FROIDCHAPELLE
COUVIN
CHIMAY
SIVRY - RANCE
HONELLES
FLOBECQ
ELLEZELLES
FRASNES - LES - ANVAINING
MONT DE L'ENCLUS
PECQ

FLANDERS

SUMMARY

Up until 1960, responsibility for rural development policy in Flanders was divided among various sectors with a leading role for agriculture. Subsequently, the diversification of the rural economy led to an even broader variety of economic expansion policies by central and local government. In the absence of overall territorial planning strategies, policy responses to rural economic change was unco-ordinated. The establishment of the region in 1980, with substantive power — including land development and physical planning — led, in 1983, to the decision by the Flemish Regional Administration to pursue an integrated rural development policy, based on broad institutional partnerships. A prime example is the transformation of the experience gained with the multi-partner land consolidation and with management bodies into a Flemish Land Institute proposed in 1988. This broad objective is to promote integrated rural development, based on comprehensive territorial planning. Area-specific projects are defined with a variety of public and private partners and are monitored by a multidisciplinary staff.

INTRODUCTION

In the past, responsibility for rural development policy has been split among various sectors. Up to 1960, agriculture played the leading role, since the other sectors were almost unrepresented in most rural areas. Although rural development was largely an autonomous process, central government took an active part in the improvement of farm structures, improvement and maintenance of watercourses (agricultural water control) and forest management. The rural development activities of provincial and local authorities were generally confined at this time to the upkeep of watercourses of local importance.

In the period 1955–60 growing awareness at international, national and local levels prompted several initiatives with significant implications for rural development. At the international level, the creation of the European Economic Community speeded up the modernisation of the agricultural sector. At the national level an agricultural investment fund was established to encourage investment in farms.

An active policy of economic expansion was adopted in rural areas, involving the creation and development of industrial estates and incentives for industrial, craft, trade or service enterprises. This policy was mainly run by inter-communal bodies and central government, and the traditional rural sector — agriculture — was rarely brought in as a partner in the formulation and implementation of these policies, which resulted in a fundamental change in rural areas in the centre of the Flemish region and in the vicinity of the cities, towns and large communes.

An active policy of subsidised housing construction was also undertaken at the same time, as a result of which most of the population could afford to buy or rent comfortable accommodation.

The above–mentioned sectoral measures, together with the modernisation and extension of the infrastructure and the democratisation of education, have resulted in considerable changes in rural areas. Initially, there were no overall territorial planning strategies and the changes were unco–ordinated. Since 1980 the Flemish Region has statutory physical development plans governing land use.

All the measures taken in the different sectors considerably increased the prosperity of the rural regions.

However, the fact that all these projects were being implemented by different partners without inter–sectoral consultation and co–ordination frequently resulted in land being wasted, in both agricultural and forested areas and areas of natural or other interest. The result was, in many cases, a drop in the quality of life.

REGIONALISATION

After a transitional period of five years, the Belgian Parliament invested the Regions which had been established in 1980 with a first set of substantial powers, covering physical planning, housing, economic expansion, rural development, the environment, etc. The institutional restructuring that ensued, and the creation of a Flemish regional administration in 1983, increased awareness of the need for a multidisciplinary and integrated rural development policy. This awareness was a significant factor in promoting consultation.

ESTABLISHMENT OF PARTNERSHIPS FOR RURAL DEVELOPMENT

The first signs of emerging partnerships for rural development are found in the laws governing the consolidation of agricultural land (1970). This measure to improve rural structures became the responsibility of a body with representatives from the public sector (Agriculture, Finance and Town and Country Planning Ministries, Provincial Governors) and the private sector (chambers of agriculture). In 1978 these teams were enlarged by the introduction of broader private sector participation and the involvement of the Ministry for Nature Conservation and the Ministry for Culture, which is responsible for monuments and sites.

The partnership system has been applied to major water control projects since 1985. The formulation and implementation of such projects is the result of teamwork among the public authorities responsible for agricultural water control, agriculture, forestry, nature conservation, fishing, the environment, regional planning, drinking water production, waste water treatment and monuments and sites and the local authorities.

In other fields partnerships exist on an ad hoc basis, but are little–developed as a systematic approach.

Decree of 21 December 1988

The new decree fulfils two objectives:

— It defines and endorses the role of *rural development* as an integrated trans—sectoral tool for improving the fabric of rural areas;
— It creates the Flemish Land Institute responsible for studying, preparing and monitoring rural development projects. This institution has a multidisciplinary staff of specialists with a range of professional backgrounds. It is also responsible for establishing a data bank on soils and a geographical data processing system.

Decisions to make the new decree operational are still in preparation; it is therefore impossible to give details of the forms of partnership used in the current reform. It is, however, certain that rural development plans will be the result of intersectoral consultation. The role of the provincial and local authorities and of the private sector is still under consideration.

NEW GUIDELINES FOR PARTNERSHIPS

Independent of the adoption of the decree of 21st December 1988, it has been decided to reinforce the partnership system for the preparation of specific rural development projects, particularly land consolidation. Alternative proposals are examined and adjusted in the light of the policies and observations of the parties concerned (regional authorities, local authorities, private sector). The final decision on the scenario to be adopted is the outcome of a cyclical planning system in which consultation with the local population plays an important part.

In the case of the Schulen rural development plan (some 2 000 ha), both the public and the private nature conservation sectors are involved in drawing up a preliminary plan for developing the ecological assets in the project. Nature conservation is thus no longer a weak partner, but a principal factor is the formulation of the overall rural development strategy for this region. This example shows that, even in the distinctly rural regions, agriculture is not always the dominant sector.

Similarly, it was decided to designate the Westhoek rural area, which is almost entirely agricultural, as a pilot project. The establishment of a motorway link to the port of Dunkirk and the channel crossing at Calais through a prime agricultural region will require consultation among all the regional and local partners with responsiblities for territorial planning, agriculture, transport, economic expansion, tourism, etc.

CANADA

SUMMARY

Rural development in Canada is a shared responsibility of several levels of government: national, provincial, local and community. Because the division of powers among levels of government is an evolving phenomenon based on constitutional interpretation and custom, rural development policy varies among the partners concerned. Given the complex nature of the challenge faced by rural areas, it is quite clear that there is often a need for co–operation and co–ordination within and among levels of government. The purpose of this summary is to provide an example of partnership both within (i.e. horizontal arrangements) and among (i.e. vertical arrangements) levels of government. It focuses on the development prospects of aboriginal communities in the Province of Québec, most of which are rural and isolated.

DEVELOPMENT POLICY FOR ABORIGINAL–PEOPLED AREAS

Aboriginal Conditions and Circumstances

There are just over 700 000 aboriginal people (registered Indians, non–status Indians, Inuits and Métis) in Canada. 10 per cent of these people live in rural Québec, in arctic, isolated and remote parts of the province. The 1981 Canadian census indicated that 41 per cent of aboriginal people have less than a grade nine education. However, there has been a dramatic increase in the number of Indians attending colleges and universities: the number has doubled in the past five years so that, today, 17 000 Indians attend post–secondary institutions. According to the 1981 census, half of the adult aboriginal population were in the labour force as compared to two–thirds of non–aboriginal people. Out–migration from aboriginal communities has remained stable: approximately one–third of Indians and Inuits live away from their communities.

Studies on the circumstances of aboriginal economic conditions have identified several barriers to economic development:

- Access to capital to finance enterprise and development;
- Lack of education, training and labour market experience;
- Isolation from major markets and transportation costs;
- Inadequate community physical infrastructure; and
- Indian Act restrictions on the use of reserve assets as business loan collateral.

Development Policy: The Memorandum of Understanding

On 30th September 1987, a Memorandum of Understanding Concerning Canada/Québec Co-operation on Native Economic Development (MOU) was signed by the Government of Canada and the Province of Québec to facilitate co-operation on aboriginal economic development. The authority of the MOU derives from provisions in the Canada–Québec Economic and Regional Development Agreement (ERDA) signed 14th December 1984. It develops a unique mechanism for co-operation on aboriginal economic development, and addresses several key issues in economic policy.

Objectives of the MOU are:
- To harmonize the policies and programmes of the two governments with respect to the economic development of aboriginal peoples, and to reduce duplication;
- To analyse obstacles to participation by aboriginal peoples (Indians, Inuit and Métis) in Québec economic life, with a view to improving their participation in the provincial economy;
- To establish better means to facilitate ongoing co-operation and joint planning among the parties involved; and
- To consult aboriginal peoples or their representatives in the development of initiatives related to the MOU.

Programme adaptation and syndication (i.e. packaging available programme assistance in order to most effectively address specific issues) are the main objectives of the MOU. Both Canada and Québec recognise that syndication is a long–term process in which all parties must be committed to the careful integration of community, social, and human resources in order to develop a strong economic base. It is also recognised that adoption of policies and programmes must occur to respond to particular rural needs and opportunities. There are several principles involved:
- The governments must aim at self–sufficiency for aboriginal peoples to minimize dependency and maximize positive developments;
- It is recognised that aboriginal people must initiate and take control of their own economies to achieve self–sufficiency;
- Self–sufficiency flows from the co–operation necessary for integrating successful economic development with social, cultural and human development.

IMPLEMENTATION OF THE MEMORANDUM OF UNDERSTANDING

The MOU was negotiated by Canada among the federal and provincial governments, Canada and aboriginal peoples, and the various government departments involved. The principles of syndication and adaptation have played a pivotal role in facilitating co–operation and harmonizing the policies of the two governments involved in the MOU. 70 managers in 29 departments and agencies (13 federal and 16 provincial) meet regularly in working groups. Co–ordination of the activities of these groups is overseen by the Co–ordinating Committee responsible for implementing the MOU.

The Co–ordinating Committee

The Canada–Québec Co–ordinating Committee is responsible for implementing the MOU. The Committee is co–chaired by the Regional Director General, Department of Indian Affairs and Northern Development (DIAND), and the Director, Secretariat for Aboriginal Affairs (Québec). The Committee, which meets four times a year, includes three federal members (DIAND, Small Business and Tourism, and Federal Economic Development Co–ordinator), three provincial members (two from the Québec Secretariat for Aboriginal Affairs and one from the Secretariat for Canadian Intergovernmental Affairs), and one *ex officio* member from the Department of Industry, Science and Technology (DIST).

In addition to its overall responsibility for implementing the MOU, the Co–ordinating Committee must submit annual progress reports to its ministers. A final report on the working groups' findings and recommendations were discussed with aboriginal peoples. Recommendations were then sent to the ministers at both the federal and provincial levels of government in May 1989.

Mobilisation of the Partners

In Québec, an Advisory Committee of aboriginal people reports to the Co–ordinating Committee and includes representatives of Québec Inuit, the Secretariat of the First Nations of Québec, the James Bay Aboriginal Development Society (Cree), Native Alliance (Métis and Non–Status Indians), and the Attikamek–Montagnais Council. The Advisory Committee advises on MOU implementation plans, working group findings and co–ordination strategies necessary for long–term policy and programme success. Aboriginal peoples were consulted from the very beginning of the MOU negotiations. The purpose of consultation was to explain the objectives of the Memorandum of Understanding and the possible benefits for aboriginal communities.

Within the government, commitments among departments were achieved through letters of support at the federal level, and by decree at the provincial level. The Minister of Indian and Northern Affairs requested and received support for the objectives of the MOU from six ministers responsible for seven subsidiary agreements under the ERDA system. The Québec government passed a Decree by the Québec Council of Ministers in 1987. These commitments to co–operate are unique to aboriginal development and represent a high degree of political will to resolve issues related to aboriginal economic development.

Working Groups

One of the most important steps in implementing the MOU was the formation of working groups to analyse gaps and barriers in existing programmes (i.e. the need for adaptation), and to study new areas of co-operation (i.e. ways of syndicating or packaging). Seven groups were established immediately after the signing of the MOU in September 1987. They have submitted their reports on seven areas of priority: business, forestry, agriculture, commercial fisheries, tourism, employment and training, and mineral resources. The working groups were formed under the MOU to analyse barriers, reduce duplication, and recommend ways to improve access by aboriginal people to existing programmes. Their mandates, as defined in the MOU objectives, were:

— to analyse and examine subsidiary agreements, ERDA systems;
— to analyse laws, regulations and programmes of both levels of government to identify barriers to development; and
— to recommend ways to improve access to the different programmes not normally accessed by aboriginal peoples.

MAJOR FINDINGS

The findings of the MOU Working Groups are: co-operation and syndication must be improved between aboriginal peoples and both levels of government; increased information on programmes other than "special" programmes must be readily available to aboriginal peoples; there is a need for human resource development (entrepreneurial training, management and business skills); ERDA subsidiary agreements were found to be unsuitable for small, isolated aboriginal communities with limited expertise, but they raised interesting possibilities in the North where the aboriginal population is the majority; and, finally, although access to programmes would remain difficult, the MOU increased the opportunities for aboriginal peoples to access non-traditional programmes.

FINLAND

SUMMARY

Finland's Rural Occupations Experiment resulted in a permanent rural occupations programme with 1989 funding levels that exceed total funding for the duration of the experiment. An intergovernmental partnership arrangement that decentralises decision–making authority constitutes the core element of this programme. The experiment demonstrated that a high level of co–operation and co–ordination was important for efficient and effective functioning of this partnership. It also demonstrated the considerable decision–making capabilities of sub–national, especially provincial, levels of government in Finland, and thus the effectiveness of a partnership that decentralises decision–making authority for addressing problems associated with local socio–economic diversity. Through its permanent rural occupations programme, Finland expects to increase its effectiveness in addressing the problem of rural employment generation.

THE RURAL OCCUPATIONS EXPERIMENT

Social and economic conditions in rural Finland are highly diverse from one area to another. The need to generate employment, however, is a common concern in most rural areas. In 1983, the Finnish government initiated the Rural Occupations Experiment, designed to address the problem of rural employment generation in the context of local socio–economic diversity. This experiment resulted in a permanent rural occupations programme. A partnership arrangement involving central, provincial and communal governments that decentralises considerable decision–making authority to the provincial level is a core element of this programme. Drawing on the Rural Occupations Experiment experience, this summary details the purpose of the programme, its organisation and operation, and several lessons learned regarding effective partnership arrangements.

75

Objectives

The Rural Occupations (jobs + self–employment) Experiment involved State subsidies for development of small–scale economic enterprises in rural areas. Its primary objective was to see whether rural inhabitants could create employment for themselves by establishing small enterprises that either complement or stand independently from existing rural occupational opportunities. The ultimate aim was to secure livelihoods on small farms and reduce rural depopulation. The subsidies were designed to promote initiative on the part of village committees, which were already active in proposing ways of improving rural livelihoods.

Another objective of the Rural Occupations Experiment was to determine the extent to which local and national authorities were capable of making allowances for rural conditions that differed from one part of the country to another.

Rationale

Finland's rural population decreased by nearly 20 per cent in the 1970s. Rural inhabitants moved to South Finland and regional population centres. The main reason for this rural depopulation was an increase in agricultural productivity that reduced the need for labour.

In the 1970s, Finnish regional policy did not apply to rural areas as such. Its main objective was to industrialise less–developed areas so as to provide employment for agricultural workers. While this regional policy succeeded in creating industrialised local and regional centres, less densely populated areas were neglected.

Finland's administrative system is highly centralised. Such a system is effective in implementing large–scale social reforms. But the problems of rural Finland became so aggravated at the start of the 1980s that the central government administration found it increasingly difficult to allow for local variations in social and economic conditions and to work out valid solutions to the problems of particular local areas. The semi–pastoral economy of Lapland, the fishing–and–farming population of the south and west coast islands, and the forested regions of eastern Finland all required their own development measures, which the central administration was unable to provide.

Better administrative co–ordination on rural development issues and programmes was also needed. Rural development depended largely on programmes of the Ministry of Agriculture and Forestry. Rural areas, however, required a far more diversified set of policies and programmes to address their social, economic and infrastructural needs. The responsibility and means to address these needs rests in the numerous ministries, including the Ministries of Transport and Communications, Social Affairs and Health, Education, and Trade and Industry. An effective rural development strategy requires policy and programme co–ordination among all of these ministries.

The Rural Development Committee

The proposal to start the Rural Occupations Experiment was made by the Rural Development Committee in 1983. This Committee had been set up to co–ordinate the work of different branches of the central government administration on rural issues, and to unify their various projects under a single entity concerned with optimising rural development.

The promotion of rural livelihoods was the main subject of discussion for the Rural Development Committee. The administrative divisions of responsibility for this issue among the Ministries of Trade and Industry, Agriculture and Forestry, and Labour and the Regional Development Fund Ltd. was unclear. Each organisation was financing rural occupations under its own system, and there were both duplications and major gaps in their funding responsibilities. Other important rural livelihoods issues included the need for increased job training and improvements to transport, housing and the social security of entrepreneurs, questions with which the authorities responsible for rural livelihoods promotion were not directly concerned.

The Committee recommended the Rural Occupations Experiment as a means of solving some of the problems involved in co-ordinating rural economic policy. The experiment provided subsidies, covering all forms of small-scale rural economic activity, as incentive for local entrepreneurs to initiate projects that have potential for increasing employment. One condition for participation in the experiment was that the entrepreneur should finance at least half of the investment. The State would finance the remainder. Agriculture was not included, because it was decided to keep the existing system of agricultural subsidies intact.

The Committee debated which branch of central government administration should assume responsibility for the experiment. The Ministry of Trade and Industry was seen as unsuitable because of its lack of experience with rural conditions, and because its technical expertise related to industry and big business. Assigning responsibility to the Ministry of Labour would, in the Committee's view, overemphasize employment. The point of the experiment was to improve livelihoods, not just to reduce unemployment. The Ministry of Agriculture and Forestry was considered to be too specialised in agriculture to take issues such as home-based industry, handicrafts, and community services adequately into account. The decision was taken to assign overall responsibility to the Prime Minister's Office, whose Planning Department was already responsible for co-ordinating regional policy as practised by different branches of the administration. In 1983 the Prime Minister's Planning Department, and responsibility for the Rural Occupations Experiment, was transferred to the Ministry of the Interior.

PROGRAMME IMPLEMENTATION

Organisation

Responsibility for implementing the experiment lay with the Ministry of the Interior, after originally resting with the Prime Minister's Office, and the provincial administrations. Since both were general administrative authorities without specific experience relating to issues associated with rural livelihoods, their main job was to organise co-operation of organisations and interests so as adequately to take into consideration their views.

The Ministry of the Interior drafted the official orders on the experiment, set aside the necessary grants in the national budget, and drew up the general instructions. It also designated the experimental areas, and distributed budgetary quotas to the provincial administrations. At this stage, it was important to ensure co-operation with government political leadership. Parliament decided on the size of the grants; the government handled the detailed adminstrative decisions.

The provincial administrations decided which projects should be assisted. The central government administration did not intervene in these decisions. Such delegation of authority was essential, because it was the only way of taking differences in local conditions adequately into account.

Partners

Partnerships among national, provincial and communal government authorities were central to operation of the Rural Occupations Experiment. Co–operation between the provincial boards and the agricultural, trade and industry, and other national authorities was specified in an official order. In addition, each province organised local co–operation independently during the experiment. All project applications were handled at the provincial level by working groups that included representatives of the agricultural, industrial, labour and fishery districts and the Regional Development Fund Ltd. These experts assessed the profitability, marketability and future of each project.

This collaboration had two results. One result was an increase of knowledge about rural occupations. The agricultural and industrial authorities came to recognise the diverse ways in which rural inhabitants could earn a living. Another result was the finding that the national district authorities imposed stricter economic criteria on the projects than provincial boards did. The provincial boards were concerned mainly with the importance of a project to the applicant and his community. They also took account of personal details, such as earlier experience, age and previous training.

Co–operation between the provincial boards and the communes involved in the experiment were important to its success. The purpose of this co–operation was to gain knowledge of local issues and needs useful in setting project priorities. Opinions issued by communal managers, enterprise promotion officers and agricultural secretaries weighed heavily in the official project assessments. In one province, elected communal officials helped assess proposed projects.

The Ministry of the Interior reported annually to the central government on the results of the experiment to ensure that the political leadership and the other ministries would be kept informed.

Projects and Subsidies

Subsidies amounting to Mk 76 million were awarded under the Rural Occupations Experiment from 1982 to 1986. During this period, the provincial boards considered 5 500 applications, and granted subsidies to 2 600 small–scale entrepreneurs in 171 of Finland's 460 local authority areas or communes. Mk 10 million was available and 33 communes were involved during the first year of the experiment. The experiment peaked in 1985, when the subsidy grant was Mk 24.5 million and 134 communes, with a total rural population of about 300 000, were involved.

The applications received by the provincial boards varied widely in their scope and nature. Nearly half related to small engineering workshops, home–based industry, handicrafts, horticulture, greenhouse cultivation and machinery repair shops. The common denominator for all projects was that they were based on utilisation of farm resources: land, machinery, soil or geology, adaptation of production premises, or skills acquired as a farmer.

As the experiment proceeded, project applications for more diverse activities were received. Applications came in for service projects such as video, photography and recording studios, electronics, tourism, accountancy and horse stabling. Many of the applicants were town–to–country migrants. Their skills and ideas came from experience gained in paid employment in non–rural areas, and the decision to move to the country was influenced by the subsidies available through the experiment.

All the subsidised projects were small. In many cases, they led to part–time work, enabling one or more members of a farm family to improve their earnings, thus making it possible for the family to continue to live in the country. Some of the subsidised projects provided full–time work.

An Intergovernmental Partnership Issue

The role of the provincial administrations in rural economic policy became a subject of debate after the Rural Occupations Experiment had been running for a few years. The communes involved in the experiment suggested that they should have responsibility for assigning project subsidies involving small sums. They considered themselves to have a better understanding of local conditions and to be closer to the local people, and thus better able to assess the economic development needs of the local area. This suggestion was rejected because it was felt that a higher authority, in this case the provincial government, would approach the matter more objectively and practise a more comprehensive rural policy. Provincial government co–operation with communes in assessing local issues and conditions for use in project priority setting was deemed sufficient for effective programme implementation.

CONCLUSIONS

The Rural Occupations Experiment increased co–operation and improved co–ordination among governmental authorities at the intermediate level, and between provincial administrations and communes. It left the central government administration with greater faith in the ability of the lower levels of government to make decisions.

Communication and administrative flexibility were important to the success of the experiment. It was found that rural inhabitants have plenty of ideas on how to create employment for themselves and improve their livelihoods. Few of them, however, are at home with "officialese" or aware of the information requirements for governmental programmes. Consequently, the government officials handling the applications had to work at communicating programme requirements clearly, and they had to exercise considerable flexibility in administering these requirements.

In practice, the provincial working groups took a positive, constructive stance in reviewing projects. They tended to look for projects' strong points instead of looking for reasons for rejecting them. Applicants usually got advice, from both communal and from provincial authorities, on how to improve their projects.

TRANSITION TO A PERMANENT PROGRAMME

The Rural Occupations Experiment ended in 1986, and a permanent programme was established. The crucial factor in the partnership arrangement under this permanent programme is that the main decisions are made at the intermediate level of government administration. Enterprise assistance has been assigned to the agricultural and industrial districts. The agricultural districts assist projects run by farms; the remaining projects are handled by the industrial districts. This assures qualified professional assessment of projects in determining the distribution of subsidies.

Under the permanent programme, provincial authorities are responsible for small–enterprise promotion. They dispose of provincial funds which they use to support experimentation and research. Out of these funds they subsidise projects run by communes, training and research establishments, private companies and other bodies. These projects can involve new methods of production, product development, marketing, and co–operation among companies.

The amount of assistance for small–scale enterprises has grown substantially since the Rural Occupations Experiment ended. The national budgetary grants at the disposal of agricultural and industrial districts in 1989 are more than twice as great as the combined total during the five years since the experiment was first initiated. The funds available to provincial governments in 1989 are also greater than the total sum available during the course of the experiment.

FRANCE

SUMMARY

Negative development trends appearing in French rural areas have made it necessary to approach rural policy in a new way. This new approach was formulated in the *Contrats de Plan* established between the central and regional governments for the period 1989–1993. The Ministry of Agriculture and Forestry experimented with this new rural development approach, which is based on analysis of the economic environment. It focuses on the comparative advantages of a region and uses selective programming to emphasize competitive activities instead of simply aiding ailing sectors. New partners have been brought into the process of planning and implementing these rural development schemes, which are territorially based. In each region, civil servants, elected local officeholders, business associations, economic actors, assisted by consultancy firms, take stock of the activities that can be built on and devise development strategies concerning them. The objective is to create synergies between civil servants and producers, manufacturers and businessmen. This new strategic approach takes a comprehensive view of rural development and smooths the way for multisectoral policies. By bringing all the partners together, it helps the relevant authorities to design and implement rural development programmes that are more effective because they are more selective.

INTRODUCTION

The Transformation of Rural Areas

In the 1970s, the French authorities launched a series of local development programmes. These programmes, frequently sectoral and aimed at the modernisation of agriculture, established parterships among local authorities and provided them with assistance, first from central government and later, after decentralisation in 1982, from regional authorities. However, demographic and economic balances in rural areas changed. By 1995 barely 15 per cent of countrydwellers will be farmers, against

81

50 per cent in 1962. This demographic trend is compounded by economic restructuring, in a fundamentally changing environment. These changes make a new, truly intersectoral approach to rural development essential, one that is based on economic development programmes on a new scale of intervention. This chapter explains what is meant by "a new approach" to rural policy and gives an account of the Ministry of Agriculture and Forestry's experiment with institutional partnership schemes based on strategic development choices, with special reference to the Poitou–Charentes experiment.

A NEW APPROACH TO RURAL POLICY

More than one–third of France's entire territory is in demographic and economic decline, involving essentially rural areas. It is likely that over the next ten years the economic fabric of these areas will deteriorate as farmers and rural businessmen retire in large numbers.

Broadly speaking, these areas are:

— Those that have already been in structural decline for several years, where aging populations and out–migration increasingly result in depopulation;
— Those where farming still predominates and economic activity will have to be diversified as reforms under the common agricultural policy come into force.

In a changing economic climate where competition is becoming increasingly fierce, revitalising these areas requires significant economic development capitalising on their most dynamic assets, coupled with classical town and country programmes. This calls for a new approach to the economy of a given territory and involving new partners and new, well–targeted development approaches, grounded in a comprehensive development strategy.

A New Approach to the Economy of a Given Territory

It is now clear that classical local development frameworks are too narrowly defined for economic development to take place. To be effective, schemes must involve populations of at least 30 000 to 50 000 people and a sufficient potential in terms of farms and businesses. Nor can schemes be confined to declining areas alone. The area concerned must include a network of large villages, small towns and thriving districts to serve as poles of development. Programmes are therefore increasingly designed on the basis of areas possessing sufficient economic and human potential. Resources must be concentrated on activities that are competitive instead of being allocated, as in the past, to unprofitable or ailing sectors only.

Rural policy is based on four main elements:

— Settlement of a young working population and the transfer or take–over of farms and businesses;
— Reorganising public and private services to business and to the general public, and easing access to them;
— Expanding tourism in areas where there is real potential for this;
— Adjusting agricultural production systems, improving co–ordination between upstream and downstream activity and developing new ways of managing rural space.

Using New Insights

As an aid in decision–making, *the strategic approach*, based on analysis of markets and comparative competitivity, is a powerful instrument for assessing a region's assets. The first step is to weigh the area's strengths and weaknesses given its economic environment so as to define the strategic directions for its development. This makes it possible to selectively target programmes to support avenues that are promising given comparative advantages with respect to other regions' competition.

The very design of the programmes concerned requires considerable investment in intangibles. The introduction of specific market studies, the generalised provision of consultancy services, and the development of targeted research permitting studies of new ways of managing rural space are all equally necessary but require efforts to train partners and to make information available to them.

New Partners

The closest co–operation of all partners is essential to the success of a new approach. Central and local government, business circles and associations have become associated in a process which functions in the context of European rural policy.

Since the enactment of legislation on decentralisation in 1982 and 1983, rural development has become an issue for a variety of levels of government:

— The *commune*, concerning the management of its own territory and neighbourhood facilities;
— The *département*, concerning contributions to infrastructural equipment and territorial planning of rural areas;
— The region, concerning economic planning and development;
— Central government, as a partner in implementing rural policies.

The partnership has to be extended to include local economic actors. Only if production can be better matched to downstream demand will agriculture be able to adjust to economic change.

Every strategy to tackle rural problems presupposes coherence among the actions undertaken by individual actors in their own realm. This can be ensured by promoting contractual arrangements and multi–annual development programmes. Such arrangements have been put in place in France, where the State/Region Planning contracts for 1989–1993 were negotiated.

The European Economic Community is going to play an important part in the definition of agricultural policy and regional development programmes, especially since the doubling of Structural Funds in February 1988 with a view, amongst other things, to "promoting the development of rural areas" (Objective 5b).

THE EXPERIMENT OF THE MINISTRY OF AGRICULTURE AND FORESTRY

Starting in 1988, the elaboration of such programmes has been tried out in three pilot areas, at the initiative of the Ministry of Agriculture and Forestry, together with

83

local partners. These areas are: the "eastern arc" of the Poitou–Charentes region, "Central Burgundy" and Lozère in the Languedoc–Roussillon region.

A Strategic Approach

The pilot areas hired assistance from consultancy bureaux on:

— Defining a development strategy for the territory selected;
— Formulating a multi–annual programme in line with the strategic choices made;
— To train the economic actors concerned (civil servants, elected local office-holders and entrepreneurs) in this kind of approach, by associating them with work on the action programme.

The partnerships were established at three levels. A national steering committee comprising representatives of the ministries and business associations concerned is responsible for co–ordinating overall development orientation for the three pilot sites. At the regional level, steering committees comprising local authorities, the private sector and central government determines strategic goals and the requisite action. At local level, farmers and businessmen and representatives of central and local government co–operate with the consultancy bureau responsible for designing and formulating the development strategy.

The new approach entails, in fact, taking a strategic, businesslike approach to a rural area in difficulty, an area that must be large enough to allow the implementation of an economic policy. The consultancy bureau must:

— Draw up an exhaustive list of all the assets of the area given domestic and European competition;
— Put forward several reasoned proposals for development strategies;
— Establish a list of priorities for co–ordinated action.

Finally, the bureau must devise a system for monitoring the development scheme.

THE ESTABLISHMENT OF A PARTNERSHIP PROGRAMME
IN POITOU–CHARENTES

The Strategic Approach

The decision to follow a strategic approach in Poitou–Charentes was taken at a meeting held in April 1988, chaired by the representative of central government in that region and attended by elected officials from regional, departmental and local governments and representatives of professional organisations and regional government administrations. Representatives of regional business associations and local government officials were jointly mandated to choose, with the aid of a consultancy bureau, the economic activities that best lent themselves to development.

In the light of the study carried out, eight activities were selected: beef and sheepmeat production, construction and public works, mining and quarrying, timber production and sawmills, furniture, tourism and services to the public. Consideration of the way in which these activities could be run was followed by a breakdown into *segments* according to relations with other activities both upstream and downstream as far as the end consumer, via all the intermediary stages. Each segment represented a "product–customer" pair. Research on markets and comparative competitivity, as well as the strengths and weaknesses of the area, was then carried out for each segment.

In this way the strategic approach shed light on the different segments and showed which activities had built-in advantages for the area, which ones were under threat because of unfavourable economic conditions and which ones had development potential.

This analysis was completed for each segment by an assessment of its impact on employment and rural equilibrium. A final choice was then made and priority given to livestock production (cattle and sheep) for meat, timber production and sawmills, and tourism. Other activities (mining and quarrying, construction and public works) were not chosen because it was difficult to affect them through public policies. The remaining activity, services to the general public, is clearly considered basic to revitalisation of the territory but insufficiently worked out.

The Strategic Objectives

Overall, the strategic approach confirmed that production in the area under consideration is largely confined to primary goods with little value–added and that the area in fact possesses few of the assets required in order to compete in other activities. Therefore, it would be best to maintain or raise the competitiveness of the most promising among the primary production sectors. This means:

— Understanding better the market downstream and gaining a foothold there;
— Improving marketing and supplying products for which there is a demand;
— Turning existing quality potential to best account, at all levels, in each of the sectors selected.

A second stage in the operation of the Poitou–Charentes partnership began in March 1989, when the best way to act on the strategic choices was decided, organisational structures set up and the people best able to carry out the operation selected.

GERMANY

SUMMARY

In view of the importance of rural areas in Germany, their development is promoted in a variety of ways, with state assistance provided by the Federation and the *Länder*. Agriculture and forestry are no longer in a position to provide rural areas as a whole with a viable economic basis. German rural policy therefore focusses on rural areas in their entirety, and considers the creation in rural areas of opportunities for employment outside agriculture to be of the utmost importance. Rural development programmes were set up, involving partnerships between the Federation and the *Länder*. These partnerships are based on joint work and a sharing of financial responsibilities. Three major examples are those developed for the improvement of the agrarian structure and coastal protection, the improvement of the regional economic structure and the development of towns and villages in rural areas.

INTRODUCTION

The Importance of Rural Areas

The following figures for the Federal Republic of Germany highlight the important role played by rural areas:

— Agriculture and forestry use 80 per cent of the area of the Federal Republic of Germany;
— 50 per cent of the population lives in rural areas;
— 5 per cent of all employed persons work in agriculture and forestry;
— Agriculture and forestry account for 2 per cent of gross value added.

While it is true that the characteristic appearance of large sections of the Federal Republic of Germany is still determined by rural areas and by the agriculture and forestry activities in these areas, agriculture and forestry are no longer in a position to provide rural areas as a whole with a viable economic basis.

A policy for rural areas must therefore not confine itself to solving the present problems of agriculture and forestry; it must view rural areas in their entirety, taking into account the fact that most people are employed outside agriculture and forestry.

87

In view of this situation in rural areas, the creation of employment opportunities outside agriculture for dependent and independent employment is of the utmost importance. However important employment outside agriculture may be for rural areas, the possibilities for the State to exert direct influence here are unfortunately limited. The free market economy makes its decisions not only according to state assistance, but above all according to its expectations for the future. State measures must therefore be more strongly geared to the improvement of general economic conditions, especially the infrastructure closely related to the economy of rural areas.

In view of the growing importance of "soft" locational factors — quality of life, educational and leisure facilities and the environment — it cannot be a matter of reconstructing typical urban infrastructures and exporting the town to the countryside, but of providing rural areas with an infrastructure which will make them an interesting location for business in the future.

The development of rural areas is promoted in a variety of ways with state assistance provided by the Federation and the *Länder*. The assistance measures that are of particular importance for rural areas include the joint tasks "Improvement of the agrarian structure and coastal protection" and "Improvement of the regional economic structure", and financial assistance known as "Urban development assistance".

INSTITUTIONAL PARTNERSHIPS

"Joint Tasks" and financial assistance are particular forms of institutional partnership between the Federation and the *Länder* which are laid down in the Constitution and whose constitutional, administrative and financial aspects will not be dealt with here in detail.

Partnership for the Improvement of the Agrarian Structure and Coastal Protection

One of the particularly important Joint Tasks for rural areas is the improvement of the agrarian structure and coastal protection, which is aimed at increasing the attractiveness and economic strength of rural areas through efficient agriculture and forestry geared to future requirements, and also at facilitating their incorporation into the Common Market of the European Communities.

A major objective of agrarian structural policy is the promotion of agriculture in disadvantaged areas at locations which are predominantly structurally weak and unfavourable from an agricultural point of view.

Other priority areas are water management measures, measures to improve cultivation and measures connected with individual enterprises as well as the reallocation and consolidation of agricultural land holdings, the voluntary exchange of land and coastal protection. In the field of water management, the funds are concentrated on forward–planning measures to maintain the quality of human life: sewage treatment plants, plants for providing drinking water in rural areas, etc.

Within the framework of the promotion of investment in individual agricultural enterprises, an agricultural credit programme was introduced for the first time in 1984 with the aim of rationalising, reducing costs and easing the strain of work in agricultural enterprises.

The cost–reducing effects of the reallocation and consolidation of agricultural land holdings benefit agricultural enterprises of all sizes. In addition to this, in the case of more recent land organisation procedures, measures to improve nature conservation and those aimed at achieving a more constructive landscape conservation are increasingly being implemented.

With regard to financing, the Federation reimburses each *Land* for the expenditure incurred in implementing the Framework Plan at a rate of 60 per cent for measures to improve agrarian structure and 70 per cent for coastal protection measures.

The budgetary funds provided jointly by the Federation and the *Länder* for the improvement of the agrarian structure and coastal protection have been regularly increased in the course of the last few years and amounted in 1988 to DM 2.4 billion, of which DM 1.5 billion is provided by the Federation.

Partnership for the Improvement of the Regional Economic Structure

Another important Joint Task for rural areas is the improvement of the regional economic structures. This Joint Task serves to create new attractive and high–quality jobs and to secure existing employment. In addition to the promotion of the business sector when enterprises are set up, expanded, converted or rationalised, it is intended to extend the infrastructure closely associated with the economy and to provide services for industrial areas, extend communications, energy and water supply plants, sewage and waste disposal plants and public tourist facilities, as well as to set up training and further education facilities.

The assistance is granted on a territorial basis and, as a matter of principle, it is only granted in those areas whose economic strength is, or is in danger of falling considerably below the national average, or in which predominant economic sectors are threatened by structural change in such a way that substantial negative repercussions are occurring or are foreseeable for the area.

The improvement of the regional economic structure covers, in particular, economically weak rural and semi–rural regions, and with the aid of its investment–oriented promotional instruments has considerably strengthened regional economic growth in rural aresa. High unemployment figures in the old industrialised areas, which are particularly affected by economic structural change, have in recent years made state assistance necessary in those regions as well.

The expenditure on this joint task is shared equally by the Federation and the *Länder,* who provided a total of DM O.8 billion in 1988 for the improvement of the regional economic structure.

Partnership for the development of towns and villages in rural areas

One of the most important forms of financial assistance is that provided by the Federation to promote urban development, which, in spite of its somewhat misleading designation, is not exclusively geared to urban regions but also serves the preservation and further development of the fabric of built–up sites and the viability of towns and villages in rural areas.

Urban and village renewal is increasingly gaining in importance for the improvement of infrastructure and employment in rural areas. It serves not only to improve housing, working and living conditions and to preserve and maintain living settlement structures, but also to provide locational security and to strengthen agriculture, small businesses, small craft industries and retail trade. In this area in particular, tasks relating to agrarian structures and urban development complement each other.

A shift of emphasis towards village renewal has therefore been taking place in urban development assistance in the course of the last few years. Thus, about 57 per cent of all urban redevelopment measures promoted in the programme year 1987 concern rural areas.

The financial assistance to promote urban development has been provided by the Federation in varying amounts since 1971 and amounted in 1988 to DM 0.7 billion. Togther with the complementary funds provided by the *Länder* and the Communes, some DM 2 billion have made available annually for urban development assistance in the above-mentioned years.

Village renewal is supported by reforms in construction law. The Federation's Construction Law Code, which was enforced on 1st July 1987, has made building in rural areas easier and has considerably simplified village renewal.

GREECE

SUMMARY

In Greece, traditional sectoral and regional policies have generally not been effective in addressing rural development problems from a global perspective. In 1985, the Greater Area of Amvrakikos was selected as the location for experimenting with the planning contract approach to formulating and implementing rural development policy. The Amvrakikos Planning Contract involves a partnership among central government and local authorities and private sector interests. It places a premium on local self–reliance and involves decentralisation of responsibility and authority for development planning and policy. It fosters formulation of comprehensive, cross–sectoral policies and programmes which are specifically tuned to local development needs and potentials. Experience to date in the Amvrakikos area suggests that planning contracts are viable mechanisms for formulating and implementing rural development policies.

Historically, rural development concerns in Greece have been addressed through regional development policy. Regional policy, however, has had limited effectiveness in fostering positive socio–economic change in rural areas. Today, development plans and policies address rural development issues more directly and explicitly than in the past. In particular, Greece is experimenting with contractual policy, specifically planning and development contracts, as a mechanism for formulating and implementing rural policy.

CONTRACTUAL POLICIES —
PLANNING AND DEVELOPMENT CONTRACTS: A NEW INSTITUTION

Contractual policy and planning and development contracts belong to a complex of institutional measures promoted by the Greek State during recent years. These measures are designed to enhance participation of an ever–increasing range of representative agencies of the population in social, political and development procedures, at

91

various levels. This trend is reflective of the policy to decentralise governmental authority to the regional and local levels, now being implemented in various forms: development of local government authorities, creation of prerequisites for public participation in production procedures, creation of local administration at the regional level, creation of modernisation mechanisms, legislating the regional level by instituting the Secretary–General and the Regional Council, systematic devolution of authority to the regional and prefectural levels from central government, and institutionalising regional planning.

These changes are grounded in the following legislation: Law 1416/1984 relating to the "amendment and supplement of the provisions of the municipal and community legislature for the enhancement of decentralisation and the strengthening of local government", and Law 1622/1984 relating to "local government authorities, regional development and democratic planning". Both laws, which cover the major institutional adjustments already mentioned, refer particularly to planning contracts. Article 11 of Law 1416 clearly provides for the drawing–up of planning contracts between local authorities and public sector agencies, co–operatives, chambers of commerce and public sector scientific agencies for research, programme development and execution, and provision of services.

The institution of planning contracts leads to:

— Better co–ordination of agency activities;
— Securing of an equal co–operation between the contractual parties (e.g. between a minister and a mayor);
— Equal and reciprocal responsibility for achievement of a goal;
— Decentralisation of political power;
— Social consensus achieved by participation and utilisation of social agencies — social partners (municipal enterprises, unions, co–operatives, chambers, etc.) which could be "third contractual parties" to a planning contract; and
— Enhancement and strengthening of democratic planning procedures.

In Greece, a planning contract is considered a frame–agreement among public sector agencies, local authorities and other agencies implementing economic policy which could include private sector agencies as well. The planning contract policy actually implements a binding contract for the partners involved as regards individual medium–term planning activities. Planning contracts include initiatives relating to:

— Investment policy;
— Prices and incomes policy as well as state procurements;
— Research and technology;
— Working relations and employment issues;
— Trade; and
— Regional development policy, especially in the context of concrete geographical spaces.

This latter objective is also very important since regional policy has highest priority in Greece as a mechanism for achieving income and production convergence on an inter–regional as well as an intra–regional basis. To the extent that "region" is identified with "rural space", planning contract policy provides an obvious connection between regional development and the restructuring of rural space. The planning contract for the "development and protection of the environment of the Amvrakikos Gulf" is one of the most interesting of all contracts focusing on rural space signed to date.

THE AMVRAKIKOS GULF PLANNING CONTRACT

The Amvrakikos Gulf

The Amvrakikos Gulf lies off the northwest coast of Greece and is part of the Ionian Sea. The Greater Area of Amvrakikos includes portions of three prefectures: Preveza to the northwest, Arta to the northeast and east, and Aetoloakarnania to the east and south. The population of the area has been stable at least since 1961: it decreased by 0.72 per cent from 1961 to 1971, and increased 1.6 per cent from 1971 to 1981. The majority of the population is older, most people are near or at retirement age. Population density is quite low compared to the national average.

The economy of the Amvrakikos area is weak. 30 to 40 per cent of the labour force is employed in the tertiary sector, mostly in commercial activities servicing local markets as opposed to tourism. About 10 per cent of the labour force is employed in the secondary sector, and the remainder works in agriculture. The economic performance of agriculture has not been satisfactory, mainly due to land shortages and inadequate access to markets in the rest of the country.

Despite the depressed state of the local economy, the natural resource base of the Amvrakikos area possesses two important attributes. First, several scarce biotopes of world—wide significance are found in the area. Second, the Amvrakikos Gulf has a large aquaculture potential which has been neglected in the past.

The Planning Contract

For the Amvrakikos area to prosper, the priority issue was clear. It was necessary to develop a coherent, integrated approach to development. This approach had to reflect the full array of development targets and their interdependence. Balancing economic development and environmental protection, for example, was a must. Furthermore, decisions regarding development in the Amvrakikos area had to be based on detailed, current, and comprehensive information.

Numerous public and private sector agencies and organisations provided information and analyses describing the social, economic and ecological characteristics and problems of the Amvrakikos area. Overall information management for development planning purposes was primarily a central function. The Center of Planning and Economic Research (KEPE) played the lead role at the central level in analysing, synthesising and managing available data and information. KEPE is institutionally separate from, but under the supervision of the Ministry of National Economy. Other central government ministries contributing to data analysis and information management were the Ministry for Environment, Urban Planning and Public Works, the Ministry of Agriculture, and the Ministry of National Economy. In addition to these central government ministries, other public sector organisations, notably the Agricultural Bank of Greece and the Hellenic Bank for Industrial Development, provided important information and analysis pertaining to the Amvrakikos area.

Several private sector actors also provided information useful in planning development policy for Amvrakikos. The co—operative unions representing farmers and fisherman gave a valuable picture of social and economic conditions in the area. The local chambers of commerce contributed little, but this was expected because of the "distance" between their economic interests in the already developed areas of Greece and the situation in the Amvrakikos area.

At the end of 1984, based on all available information and analyses, KEPE prepared a preliminary development plan for Amvrakikos. This plan emphasized environmental protection, aquaculture and mild tourism development, It recommended only small and mid–scale industrial development. This preliminary plan was used as a starting point and guide in finalising a development policy strategy for Amvrakikos and the planning contract arrangement.

In March 1985, 28 central and local government agencies and local private sector representatives agreed on and signed the planning contract. The co–contracted members shared a wide range of responsibilities in terms of infrastructure works, development projects, pursuit of productive investments, development finance and credit facilities. Moreover, the members were mutually bound to respect and strictly apply ecological protection restrictions governing their actions.

Planning contracts are grounded in the principles of decentralised planning and administration. A planning contract is designed to provide an institutional framework which enhances local capacity to develop and utilise local resources. Following this principle, the Planning Contract for Amvrakikos leaves considerable margin for adapting the original development strategy to changing local needs, while at the same time keeping that strategy within the targets and scope of the current national five–year plan.

The Amvrakikos Gulf Development Agency (ETANAM)

One of the objectives of the planning contract was the setting up of the Amvrakikos Development Agency (ETANAM), in accordance with the provisions of Article 44 of Law 1416/84. ETANAM's responsibility is the implementation of the Amvrakikos development programme. Specifically, the Agency's purpose is to provide services in sectors in which local resources are inadequate and to engage in activities of all kinds which will further the aims of the planning contract. In addition, the Agency undertakes the design, co–ordination and monitoring of projects included in its five–year plans and assigned to it by special programme contracts. It also plans special development programmes and supports local development initiatives. In effect, ETANAM is the lever to mobilise the productive potential of the area, the agency to provide technical support for local productive initiatives and the catalyst to promote endogenous development.

The duration of the Agency is 50 years, and it is in the legal form of a municipal and co–operative joint–stock company (SA) with a share capital of 45 million drachmas, divided between ordinary and preference shares. Of the ordinary shares, 41 per cent are held by local government authorities (LGAs), 39 per cent by co–operative organisations and 20 per cent by public sector organisations. The three prefectural funds own 75 per cent of the preference shares and the remaining 25 per cent is divided among the Agricultural Bank of Greece, the Hellenic Industrial Development Bank and the Consignments and Loans Fund. The Agency is to be administered by an eleven–member Board.

The effectiveness of ETANAM depends on two quite distinct parameters:

— The degree to which its organisation and administration are rational, enabling it to mobilise local productive potential; and

— The degree to which it receives long–term and meaningful support from agencies in the public, private and social sectors.

The basic targets of the ETANAM's plan of action include environmental protection, fish farming, tourism, farming and stock breeding, manufacturing and services. Promotion of technological development will play a primary role in ETANAM's plan of action, as a way to encourage local innovation.

Within the context of these basic targets, ETANAM provides an array of services. These services address the needs and interests of entrepreneurs, public sector agencies, and local organisations. In addition, ETANAM has the freedom to investigate, formulate and promote special development initiatives focusing on such issues as aquaculture, tourism and environmental protection.

The founding of ETANAM is the outcome of the joint political will of the State and the local agencies who hold a decisive part of its share capital. The nature of ETANAM's strategic goals give it the character of a technical organisation which operates in association rather than competition with the specialised organisations of the public and private sectors of the economy. The framework for the operation of ETANAM offers the following advantages:

— Its legal form permits operational flexibility and efficiency.
— The composition of its share capital (with the exclusive participation of public sector organisations, local government and social agencies and organisiations) permits direct democratic social control over its activities and ensures it the greatest possible consensus and systematic support on the part of the State, local government authorities, co–operatives, Chambers of Commerce and other bodies;
— The representative composition of the Board of the Agency permits an internal blend of the various social and political approaches;
— Its organisational flexibility will help it play the part of an effective tool in directing external inputs into the endogenous development process;
— The private economy framework within which the Agency operates allows a rational connection between planning for development and development initiatives.

THE AMVRAKIKOS GULF PLANNING CONTRACT EXPERIENCE

The Amvrakikos Planning Contract experience gives rise to several considerations relating to the effective organisation and functioning of this new partnership arrangement. Three particularly important considerations inlcude participation of public and private sector actors, intergovernmental relations, and programme finance.

There are a number of possible forms of co–operation between public and private sector actors which could be mutually acceptable, and at the same time enhance the effectiveness of programme implementation. It is important to continually seek out these alternative forms. Private sector organisations, such as banks and chambers of commerce, for example, could participate more broadly in rural development programmes for the Amvrakikos area and still benefit financially. The public sector, on the other hand, could be more pragmatic in pursuing its administrative and social responsibilities, and in doing so help to maximise benefits and minimise costs (in terms of the state budget and fluctuating items of public expenditure).

A second concern is relations among different levels of the public administration. The effectiveness of the planning contract partnership presupposes a high degree of intergovernmental co–ordination and flexibility in undertaking, rapidly assessing and promoting programme initiatives. The Amvrakikos development programme incorporates the central and regional governments as integral parts of the 'developing' area, not neutral exogenous factors. Increased intergovernmental co–operation could enhance the effective functioning of the planning contract partnership.

The issue of financing the planning contract partnership is a key consideration. Adequate programme funding is necessary to ensure that the development potentials of the Amvrakikos area are maximised. Adequate funding hinges on securing available external funds, such as Integrated Mediterranean Programme funds. It also hinges on achieving a considerable degree of self–financing, a primary goal of the Amvrakikos development programme.

The Amvrakikos Planning Contract has led to considerable qualitative improvement in socio–economic and environmental conditions, given the problems which had to be dealt with. The most important achievement, however, is that this new approach to regional development policy and programme implementation has been accepted by the multiple partners involved.

IRELAND

SUMMARY

Ireland is experimenting with a novel integrated rural development programme. This programme is grounded in the principle that economic development in rural communities and areas should reflect local ideas and be a local responsibility. The programme calls for a Core Group, a partnership of community group representatives, local leaders and other individuals, to assume this responsibility for local development areas. Through this programme, Ireland hopes to revive and strengthen its rural areas, and thus enhance the social and economic well–being of the nation as a whole.

THE INTEGRATED RURAL DEVELOPMENT PROGRAMME

Rural development is an important part of Ireland's strategy to strengthen its national social and economic well–being. The Irish Government has initiated an integrated rural development programme grounded in the principle that development should reflect primarily the ideas and initiative of local people. The key element in implementing this programme is the Core Group, a partnership of representatives of community voluntary organisations, local community leaders and other individuals who take responsibility for rural community and economic development in their local areas. This programme has been introduced on an experimental basis in selected areas as a way of gaining the experience necessary to implement it effectively nationwide. In describing the pilot programme, this summary details the principles, objectives and operational characteristics of Ireland's integrated rural development programme.

Objectives

The Irish Government, as part of its overall Programme for National Recovery, decided on the introduction of a special measure to revive and strengthen rural areas. This goal is to be achieved by stimulating rural enterprise so as to provide more employment and income opportunities, fostering a sense of community identity among people in rural areas, and improving the quality of rural life. The intention is to create a viable self–sustaining rural population.

The strategy underlying the Irish programme is grounded in two principles:

1. to bring about greater involvement of local people in the economic, social and cultural development of their own areas; and
2. to encourage them to decide upon their own set of development priorities and to accept the responsibility for bringing their own aspirations to reality. The emphasis is on fostering viable private and community enterprises based on full utilisation of the abilities and talents of local people.

Rationale

As measured by socio–economic indicators of comparative well–being, Ireland as a region is the sixth poorest in the Community of 12. This comparative disadvantage is predominately rural–based. Two–thirds of the population, outside Dublin, live in rural areas, and some 15 per cent of the population is directly employed in farming. Opportunities for non–farm employment are limited, unemployment rates are high (up to 23 per cent) and emigration is a major problem. Agricultural holdings consist almost entirely of small owner–operated family farms. The preservation of these holdings is a central objective of Government policy.

At the same time, the agricultural sector as a whole suffers from major structural difficulties, resulting in low average incomes and serious under–employment on many farms, especially in the less–developed Western region of the country. These difficulties, allied to the shortage of non–farm employment, are major contributing factors to the continuing migration from rural areas and their consequent decline. The current market restrictions, arising from the changed orientation of the European Community's Common Agricultural Policy, tend only to exacerbate the situation, and there is an obvious need to diversify the agricultural and rural economy so as to provide additional income and employment outlets.

PROGRAMME IMPLEMENTATION

Pilot Programme

For the purpose of gaining the experience necessary to embark on a nationwide programme, it was decided that the new measure should be introduced in all of its dimensions on an experimental basis. A team of qualified professional consultants were engaged to assist in the design and implementation of this pilot programme.

Twelve pilot areas were selected to be involved in the programme for a period of two years. Each area is a small cohesive socio–economic unit, with a population varying in size from about 5 000 to 10 000 people. While each area has its own particular natural advantages, traditions and economic strengths, the aim was to select areas which would be broadly representative of other areas in the country. Thus, if the programme is successful in one of the pilot areas, it will stand a good chance of being successful elsewhere when the programme is eventually undertaken nationwide.

The Co-ordinator

In each pilot area, a special Co-ordinator was appointed and given the task of assisting and facilitating the local community's area development efforts, in close liaison with existing advisory and developmental services and with local voluntary organisations. The people appointed possessed special qualities, such as innovation, energy, leadership and a proficiency in inter-personal skills.

Before taking up duty in October 1988, the Co-ordinators underwent an intensive training course, conducted by the pilot programme consultants. As part of their training, they were given thorough insight into the workings of the central and regional administrations in Ireland and the European Community. In addition, they received full instruction in the principle underlying the programme, and they were advised as to the best method of stimulating the local community, identifying potential development resources (including human resources), and encouraging the effort necessary to trigger community action.

The training of the Co-ordinators is an ongoing process, carried out through monthly meetings organised by the consultants and through person-to-person contact between the individual Co-ordinators and the consultants. The intention is to organise additional co-ordinator training modules if necessary as the programme proceeds.

Partners

The first task of the Co-ordinator in each area was to organise a Core Group. This group consists of individuals and representatives of voluntary organisations committed to the development of the area and willing to make the effort necessary to bring about such development. The number of persons in a group varies from one area to another but, purely as a guide, it was recommended that the Co-ordinators consider a group of eight to ten persons as the ideal.

The Core Group is, in effect, the body responsible for the operation of the programme in each area. In the beginning, it is expected that most of the initiative for operating the programme will lie with the Co-ordinator. As the programme develops, however, and as the core groups gain experience and confidence, it is expected that the Core Group will increasingly become the dominant force in the partnership. The Co-ordinator will revert to the roles of facilitator for the Group's efforts and adviser as to how the resources of various development agencies might best be used in furthering projects selected for implementation.

Shared Learning

A basic principle of the pilot programme is that no area is left to develop in isolation from the other areas involved in the experiment. The programme is built around the notion of shared learning among all individuals and all groups involved. The Co-ordinators and Core Groups are required to visit each other at regular intervals to compare problems, discuss solutions, examine resources and assess progress and aspirations. Through such interaction, every one of the areas is "twinned" with another.

The shared learning process is brought a step further through the organisation of a series of four workshops to be held at approximately six-month intervals over the two–year period of the pilot programme. Each workshop is to be attended by all members of the Core Groups, the Co–ordinators, the consultants involved with both the training and the overall design of the programme, and by representatives of the Department (Ministry) of Agriculture and Food, the central government department sponsoring the programme.

The first of these workshops was held in November 1988. Considering that the programme had been in operation less that two months, and that the membership of the Core Groups had not been finalised in all areas, the result was remarkable and held out much hope for the success of the programme. As might be expected, much of the work discussed by programme participants was tentative and exploratory. Core Group members, for example, described their areas, their problems and their perceptions of the potential for development. Contributions were made by experts (both from Ireland and abroad) who had made special studies of rural development and by representatives of national development agencies who would be in a position to assist local communities in bringing projects to fruition. A number of informational and inspirational talks were given with a view to ensuring that the fundamental principles of the programme would be fully understood by all concerned and would be borne in mind in planning the development of the areas.

The second workshop was held in March 1989. On this occasion, the Core Groups discussed possible projects, or types of projects, which they might undertake. A number of case studies of successful community–based enterprises were presented, with a view to imparting confidence, stimulating discussion and encouraging imitation. The inspirational content of the workshop was continued, but the main emphasis was on the presentation and discussion of the plans of the Core Groups. At the end of the workshop, the Core Groups were in a better position to judge which of their envisaged projects had the greatest potential and should be implemented as an initial step in the development of their area.

Similar activities will be continued and expanded upon at the third and fourth workshops. By the time of the third workshop, a number of projects will have been undertaken in the various pilot areas and an examination of their operation and effectiveness, in a "peer–present situation", will be an important component of the workshop.

Monitoring

An independent evaluation of the pilot programme will be conducted by the Irish Economic and Social Research Institute. An Institute representative will be present at all workshops, and the Institute is kept fully informed of progress in the various pilot areas. The intention is to have a mid–term assessment prepared, as well as a final assessment, so that any necessary adjustments can be made before implementing the programme nationwide.

Funding

No special funds are being made available to finance projects implemented as a result of the programme. The aim is to ensure that more effective use is made of existing financial resources as well as the services and expertise of existing development agencies. The main expenditures under the programme will be for the Co–

ordinators' salaries and expenses, consultants' fees, and the costs of special studies undertaken by the various Core Groups.

The EC Commission is making a financial contribution to the cost of the programme. The Commission has a particular interest in the programme as it relates to Objective 5b of the priority objectives adopted by the European Community for the future operation of the Structural Funds. The report on the independent assessment will, of course, be made available to the Commission and should be of assistance to them in finalising EC integrated rural development policy under the new regime governing the Structural Funds.

CONCLUSIONS

While the operation of the pilot programme will undoubtedly result in a number of good development projects being undertaken in the various areas, the primary intention is that it should form part of an overall learning process. The underlying principle is "bottom up", i.e. development ideas will emanate from the local community and will not be imposed by central government administration, as has been the case in the past.

At this stage, therefore, it is possible only to speculate on the pilot programme's outcomes. Nevertheless, it is probably safe to assume that in most areas emphasis will be placed on small/medium rural business ventures, on-farm value-added enterprises, rural tourism and other service sector development, and amenity and social improvements.

Each of these possible programme initiatives has potential for enhancing the social and economic vitality of rural areas in Ireland. Small/medium rural business enterprises need not necessarily have links with agriculture, but could use the skills and aptitudes of everyone in the local work force. Such enterprises could encompass such undertakings as country shops, arts and crafts, fishing and mariculture. On-farm enterprises might be expected to diversify from traditional lines of production into, say, deer, rabbits, goats, fruit and non-traditional vegetables, as well as organic farming, afforestation, horse-breeding and horticulture. Rural tourism offers a very wide range of possibilities for local communities, especially as regards the provision of collective amenities and organised groups and special-interest holidays.

The Irish authorities are experimenting with this novel rural development programme with an open mind. No limit is placed on the type of project or range of activities which a Core Group may promote under the programme. The only requirement is that all such projects and activities should have as an objective the development of the area in line with the wishes of the local people.

NETHERLANDS

SUMMARY

Planning and implementation of programmes initiated under the Rural Redevelopment Act requires the involvement of numerous partners representing all levels of government, the private sector, producer associations and community groups. The effective functioning of this partnership arrangement requires broad–based political support for the rural development programmes initiated, close working relationships among the partners, and adequate financial support. The Rural Redevelopment Act was put into effect in 1979 to provide a framework for addressing the problems of structural unemployment and general economic stagnation in the East Groningen area and peat district of Groningen and Drenthe.

THE RURAL REDEVELOPMENT ACT

The social and economic vitality of rural areas is an important policy goal in the Netherlands. Over the past thirty to forty years, the area east of Groningen and the former peat district of Groningen and Drenthe, a primarily agricultural region in northeast Netherlands, has experienced high structural unemployment and economic stagnation. In 1979, the Rural Redevelopment Act was put into effect to deal specifically with the economic and social problems confronting this region. Implementation of the development plans and programmes initiated under this act requires that representatives of central, provincial and municipal government, farmers' associations, polder boards, Chambers of Commerce, environmental organisations and other groups work co–operatively as partners. This summary details the objectives of the Rural Redevelopment Act and its rationale, the key partners and their roles in programme implementation, and three factors important for the Act's effectiveness.

Objectives

The origin of the Rural Redevelopment Act stems from the application for a land consolidation project for the Peat District in 1970. The Peat District, located in the northeast part of the Netherlands near Groningen, is an area of reclaimed peatland that since the end of the 19th century has been used primarily for agricultural

103

production. During the 1960s and 1970s, the Peat District, along with two adjacent agricultural areas, the Oldambt and Westerwolde, experienced high structural unemployment and economic stagnation, due to significant decline in agriculture and other sectors of their economies.

In 1970 farmers in the Peat District presented a request for a large land consolidation project covering 70 000 hectares which they regarded as a possible solution for their problems. But, because the problems of the Peat District and the Oldambt and Westerwolde regions are interdependent and not confined solely to the agricultural sector, the government decided that these three areas together should be the object of a large–scale reconstruction or redevelopment project. After consultations with the inhabitants of these regions, the Rural Redevelopment Act was drafted for this purpose. It became effective on 1st January 1979.

The Rural Redevelopment Act has two main objectives: 1. to stimulate the economic and social development of the region and 2. to create a good living and working climate. More specifically, the Act provides for the co–ordinated and, where possible, integrated implementation of activities such as the following:

— Improvement of the infrastructure and the agricultural structure;
— Reallotment of land holdings and land–use rights;
— Provision of facilities for landscape conservation and outdoor recreation;
— Conservation and improvement of the landscape and elements of socio–cultural and historial value;
— Provision for the renewal of town and village centres, including demolition or renovation of inadequate housing; and
— Creation of public facilities for the drainage and purification of waste water.

Rationale

In earlier centuries, there was a large area of peat bog in the southeast of the province of Groningen and the neighbouring part of the province of Drenthe. These bogs were located in a broad depression created by meltwater flows after the Ice Ages. The excavation of the peat took off in the 17th century, and a dense network of canals was constructed, which served first to drain the bogs and then to transport the peat.

The city of Groningen played an important part in this development. The city acquired large areas of land, and was the owner of the roads and canals, from which it received tolls. It placed upon the peat diggers an obligation to restore the land for agriculture after they had finished digging the peat. The soil thus created was infertile in itself, but its fertility was increased first by the addition of manure and urban refuse and, from the end of the 19th century, by the addition of large quantities of artificial fertilisers. In this way, the basis was laid for a very specific agricultural region, with its characteristic geometrical pattern of canals and roads, along which villages have developed.

The reconstruction area of East Groningen and the former peat district of Groningen and Drenthe, which consists of the Peat District, the Oldambt and Westerwolde, covers an area of 130 000 hectares. It involves two provinces, includes 30 municipalities, and has approximately 275 000 inhabitants.

For a long time, East Groningen and the former peat district of Groningen and Drenthe have been facing problems which are extensive and complex by Dutch standards. Employment has disappeared entirely in the peat industry and has substantially gone down in agriculture. Since the fifties and sixties, employment in the strawboard and potato starch industries has not sufficiently compensated for the total loss of jobs, and the area has consistently had one of the highest structural unemployment rates in the Netherlands.

Although the farms in the Oldambt, the Peat District and Westerwolde are relatively large, they are still too small to provide a decent income when cultivated in the traditional manner. Especially in the Peat District, the composition and physical structure of the reclaimed soil makes it in many cases unsuitable for modern and economic farm management. Overall, the economy of the reconstruction area has been stagnating, and the average income has been substantially lower than the national average.

The provincial authorities of Groningen and Drenthe and the central government reached the conclusion that there were further problems, which were reflected in an unemployment rate (20 per cent) well above the national average of 15 per cent and an economic growth rate that lagged far behind that of all the other regions of the country. The agricultural industry had to contend not only with the general economic recession of the 1970s, but also with rising costs incurred in combatting the serious environmental pollution caused by the discharge of factory effluent into the canals. Boat building, which was once an important industry along many of the canals, had shifted to more spacious navigable water in the northeast of the province of Groningen.

Residential amenities were deficient in many respects, mainly because of the ribbon development which characterised most of the settlements and the lack of facilities for open air recreation. The presence of some 9 000 hectares of land owned by the city of Groningen also formed an obstacle to the further development of the region.

PROGRAMME IMPLEMENTATION

Partners

The execution of the Rural Redevelopment Act is entrusted to a reconstruction committee, on which there are representatives of all interested parties in the reconstruction area. This committe consists of 31 members and 29 advisors. The members include representatives of the two provinces, the municipalities, farmers' organisations, the polder boards, the Chambers of Commerce, the unions, environmental organisations and socio–cultural institutions. The advisors are representatives of different ministries and provincial authorities. The Minister of Agriculture and Fisheries provides the manpower for the secretariat of the committee. This secretariat prepares the decisions to be taken by the committee and takes care of their subsequent implementation.

The redevelopment area has been divided in seven sub–areas. Each of these areas has a working subcommittee, under supervision of the reconstruction committee. The task of each subcommittee is to prepare a redevelopment plan for its particular area. These plans are reviewed in consultation with the inhabitants of the sub–areas through an extensive public participation process, and the national and provincial governments make a formal assesment of each plan. Once a redevelopment plan is approved and established, the working subcommittee for the sub–area involved is responsible for implementing the plan.

Programme Approval and Funding

In the spring of 1980, the reconstruction committee submitted a provisional redevelopment programme for discussion and approval. After consultations this provisional programme was sent for advice to the Central Land Consolidation Committee in the autumn of 1980. This committee is now known as the Central Land Development Committee. In April 1981, this committee sent the provisional programme, along with its comments and advice, to the provincial governments of Groningen and Drenthe, who approved it in May 1983. In that period, both provincial governments negotiated with the national government about the amount of financial support to be contributed by the state for the redevelopment programme.

In December 1983, the national government approved the redevelopment programme, after having limited its scope, especially its budget. The programme contains provisions for the following initiatives:
- — Improvement of infrastructure (road and canals);
- — Land consolidation and improvement of the agricultural structure (enlargement of holdings);
- — Abolition of the ownership rights of the City of Groningen for canals, bridges, roads and land in the redevelopment area;
- — Provisions relating to the landscape, recreation, nature and historical features;
- — Renewal of the built–up areas of towns and villages;
- — Environmental improvement; and
- — Provisions to maintain or improve economic, social and cultural quality of life of the population.

The total costs of the Rural Redevelopment Project were estimated in 1980 at over 2.5 billion guilders. Urban and village renewal, agricultural improvements, and infrastructure development were the largest budget items. Central government was to contribute two–thirds of this amount, with the remainder provided by the provinces of Drenthe and Groningen, municipal governments, water control boards and the private sector. The project was also eligible for a grant from the Regional Development Fund of the European Communities.

CONCLUSIONS

The redevelopment programme for the East Groningen area and the peat district of Groningen and Drenthe covers a large geographic area, focuses on a wide range of rural development issues, and involves numerous and varied development activities. A partnership involving all levels of government, the private sector, producer associations and other interests is central to planning and implementing the programmes. Full implementation in all of the seven sub–areas will likely take ten to twenty years.

These conditions have been identified as central to the effectiveness of this programme. First, given the large geographic area and multiple issues covered by the programme, broad–based political support and participation is necessary for both preparation and implementation of development plans. Second, all partners and other programme participants must be willing to co–operate fully in the programme planning and implementation. Third, the programme and its development plans must have adequate financial support from central government and other programme partners.

Between 1979 and 1989, the first ten years that the Rural Redevelopment Act has been in effect, these conditions have been met. The programme has broad public support and involvement of numerous public and private partners, the preparation and implementation of the rural development plans has been well received, and adequate funding has been forthcoming.

RURAL DEVELOPMENT PARTNERSHIPS IN EAST-GRONINGEN AND THE GRONINGEN-DRENTHE PEAT DISTRICTS

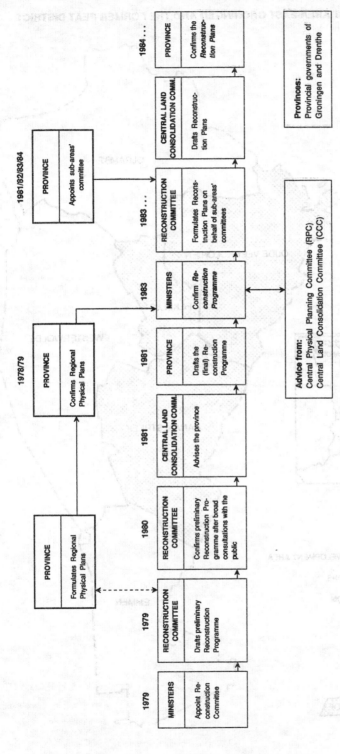

1979

MINISTERS — Appoint Reconstruction Committee

1979

RECONSTRUCTION COMMITTEE — Drafts preliminary Reconstruction Programme

1978/79

PROVINCE — Formulates Regional Physical Plans

1980

RECONSTRUCTION COMMITTEE — Confirms preliminary Reconstruction Programme after broad consultations with the public

PROVINCE — Confirms Regional Physical Plans

1981

CENTRAL LAND CONSOLIDATION COMM. — Advises the province

1981

PROVINCE — Drafts the (final) Reconstruction Programme

1983

MINISTERS — Confirm *Reconstruction Programme*

1983 . . .

RECONSTRUCTION COMMITTEE — Formulates Reconstruction Plans on behalf of sub-areas' committees

1981/82/83/84

PROVINCE — Appoints sub-areas' committee

CENTRAL LAND CONSOLIDATION COMM. — Drafts Reconstruction Plans

1984 . . .

PROVINCE — Confirms the *Reconstruction Plans*

Advice from:
Central Physical Planning Committee (RPC)
Central Land Consolidation Committee (CCC)

Provinces:
Provincial governments of Groningen and Drenthe

Ministers:
Minister of Agriculture and Fisheries
Minister of Housing Affairs and Physical Planning
Minister of the Interior
Minister of Economic Affairs
Minister of Culture, Recreation and Social Work
Minister of Traffic and Public Works
Minister of Finance

- The ministers appoint the Reconstruction Committee.
- The Reconstruction Committee drafts a preliminary Reconstruction Programme and provisionally confirms it.
- The Reconstruction Programme is to be confirmed after the Regional Physical Plans are confirmed.
- The Reconstruction Programme is to be confirmed by the ministers.
- The Reconstruction Committee formulates the Reconstruction Plan for each of the sub-areas.
- These Plans are based on the overall Reconstruction Programme and Regional Physical Plans.
- The Reconstruction Plans are to be confirmed by the province.
- The Reconstruction Committee executes the Reconstruction Plans.
- Consultations are foreseen throughout all phases of the reconstruction process.

REDEVELOPMENT AREA EAST GRONINGEN AND THE FORMER PEAT DISTRICT

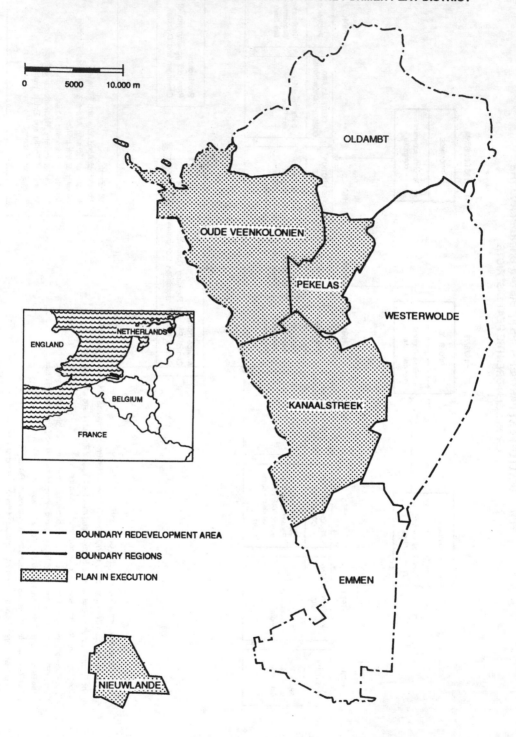

0   5000   10.000 m

OLDAMBT

OUDE VEENKOLONIEN

PEKELAS

WESTERWOLDE

KANAALSTREEK

ENGLAND
NETHERLANDS
BELGIUM
FRANCE

EMMEN

NIEUWLANDE

—··— BOUNDARY REDEVELOPMENT AREA
——— BOUNDARY REGIONS
[::::] PLAN IN EXECUTION

NEW ZEALAND

SUMMARY

The new system of local government in New Zealand is grounded in an institutional partnership that ensures accessible local government responsive to the people. Given the allocation of functions between district and regional units of government, efficient and effective governmental operations require that these units work in harmony. Their partnership must be built on compatibility and co–operation. The advantages of this institutional partnership are three–fold: it ensures the co–ordination of service delivery, encourages cost efficiency and effectiveness, and brings local and regional services to people in their communities. The institutional mechanism now in place allows for and encourages participation in community decision–making and local service delivery.

REFORMATION OF LOCAL GOVERNMENT IN NEW ZEALAND

The reformation of local government in New Zealand was achieved by the Local Government Commission without a "grand plan". The Commission, an independent statutory body, working in partnership with local government and within the bounds of its legislative mandate, fulfilled the principal reformation objective — improving New Zealand's system of local government.

The Commission's approach was flexible, seeking local initiatives and reasonable local agreements. In fulfilling its task, the Commission adhered to an operational mode built on the principles of investigation, communication and consultation. It was the Commission's expectation that through this method of shared responsibility an appropriate system of local government would evolve rather than require imposition. That expectation was fulfilled. The Commission worked in partnership with local government to evolve a new system relevant to today's needs and able to respond to future demands. The new system establishes two new levels of organisation, regional and district, within the structure of local government. Regional and district units of government are to be compatible; they are structured to be complementary, not competitive. They are, in fact, to work in partnership.

Improving Local Government

In the opinion of the Commission, improving the system of local government required:

a) A smaller number of units;

b) Managerially and technically stronger units;

c) Units which correspond with and serve existing, rather than historical communities of interest;

d) Units which can perform allocated functions in an efficient and effective manner, through wise use of limited resources and economies of scale in service administration and delivery;

e) Units which through electoral processes and service delivery techniques can be more responsible to the input and needs of local people;

f) Units which generally have multi–purpose functional capacity and responssibility;

g) Jurisdictional boundaries which so far as practicable relate the costs and benefits of particular functions to a similar community of interest.

Local Government Functions

Achieving the goal of complementary, working partnerships among regional and district unit councils required the Commission to clearly delineate their respective functions. In creating regional councils within New Zealand's unicameral system of government, central government was divesting some of its authority and responsibilities to a unit of local government with regional authority and responsibilities. Regional units have responsibility for a number of mandatory functions including land use planning and civil defence, catchment and river control, and a wide range of functions relating to the planning, management and regulation of land, sea and air resources. Service delivery is the prime function of district government.

In seeking the wise use of limited environmental resources and to avoid conflict between their management and their use, the Commission separated the planning, management and regulation function from the service delivery function. Where a complete separation was neither practical nor achievable, functional activities were placed with the regional councils. In such circumstances, the Commission expects those authorities to set the policy context but to contract with the district unit for the delivery of services.

The strict legislative requirement to have regional boundaries conform to one or more water catchments created some practical problems for the Commission. Recognising that regions and districts would include a number of different communities, it became a major responsibility of the Commission to ensure that regional and district communities of interest were not divided. Where there was difficulty in sensibly achieving commonality of regional and district concerns, the Commission used an alternative solution — the "straddle technique". This measure not only satisfied conflicting regional and district communities of interest, it also allowed regional water and soil administration to be carried out in a co–ordinated manner. The straddle technique involves placing that part of a district authority affected into two regions. District functions continue to reflect the distinct community of interest, while for water catchment purposes, district concerns would be handled within the water catchment–

defined boundary of the appropriate region, reflecting the regional community of interest and allowing the regional co–ordination of water and soil resource programmes. Such a technique can only be successfully used in instances where units of local government are complementary — where partnership prevails and where district communities of interest are clearly defined.

Local Government Partnerships

The Commission proposed that regional units of government should not dominate district units — both should be seen as organisational units working in tandem to facilitate and provide an overall system of local government. In performing their different functions, these units will need to develop and maintain close communication and co–operation. They are complementary components of the local government system. To ensure communication and co–operation, the Commission has provided for regional transition committees to meet with their opposite numbers, district transitional committees, to discuss the delegation of service delivery. These committees are to jointly devise appropriate arrangements for the physical delivery of services relating to their allocated functions. Ratepayers, as the Commission emphasised, would not be impressed unless the local government system as a whole was seen to be operating efficiently and effectively in managing the delivery of governmental services. These transitional committees are yet another tool to reinforce the institutional partnership now existing between regional and district councils.

Service centres were established by the Commission to take the lead in providing local services. Their function and operation is based on the philosophy that local government should be both easily understood and accessible to the people. They involve a partnership between local government and its constituents; they enhance the participation of local people in community service decision–making. One of the key factors underlying the establishment of service centres is to ensure that the new local government councils do not become centralised bureaucracies. The centres are designed to take the councils and their services to the people. The Commission requires also that regional and district units should seek the utilisation of the local service centre facilities for regional services and information. This requirement meets the need for efficient and effective services while giving the people local access to regional activities, information and services.

PORTUGAL

SUMMARY

Portugal's economy depends to a considerable degree on the economic and social vitality of its rural areas. This has led the Portuguese Government to promote integrated rural development policies involving public and private partners. Partners are mobilised through institutions responsible for co-ordinating, implementing and monitoring development programmes, thus providing synergy between private–sector agents, government services and the European Community. This summary describes the development programme for the Northern Alentejo.

DEVELOPMENT PROGRAMME FOR THE NORTHERN ALENTEJO

The Northern Alentejo Region

The socio–economic characteristics of the northern part of the Alentejo, which lies inland in Portugal, are similar to those of the Alentejo as a whole. Its economy is based essentially on the farm sector, and its low–income population has been moving away from the countryside. In particular, young people tend to migrate to the coastal towns or go abroad. This weakness in socio–economic structure, resulting from the deficiencies in the agricultural sector and ill–regulated industrial development, has become the target of rural policy in order to provide the area with a level of development commensurate with its potential. In fact, the region has a wide range of resources. It holds important reserves of uranium, and the finest granite in Portugal. Because of its historical heritage, cuisine, wealth of folklore and possibilities for hunting and fishing, it is also a prime tourist area. Finally, agro–food and crafts enterprises are evidence of a long–standing industrial base.

Objectives

A key objective of the Northern Alentejo development programme is to retain, and possibly increase, the population by stimulating entrepreneurial capacities in the area. To this end, three broad lines of action have been decided on:

113

- Removing the main barriers to harmonious development of economic sectors;
- Utilising the area's productive capacities and basing its economic and social development on local resources; and
- Enhancing occupational skills in order to increase local participation and vitalise local decision–making centres.

An integrated development programme has been prepared to work towards these objectives.

The Integrated Development Operation (OID)

The Co–ordinating Commission for the Alentejo and local authorities took the lead in initiating the Integrated Development Operation (OID) for the Northern Alentejo. This programme was approved by the Council of Ministers on 5th April 1986. It was prepared by a team of technical experts from the main government services, in partnership with local development agents. The central government was represented by its central or regional services, and the local councils by their mayors to ensure that the measures agreed were in line with the needs and aspirations of the local people. The private sector took part through organisations of employers and labour.

During the preparatory stage, five main lines of development were agreed upon:

i) Improving infrastructure

The Northern Alentejo has inadequate infrastructure and community facilities. This tends to stimulate outmigration; the area fails to attract productive investment needed for job creation and utilisation of available resources. Accordingly, the programme proposed to extend the water and sewage systems, and to build some 200 km of national highways and 400 km of local roads. These measures were designed to retain the local population and encourage industry settlement.

ii) Restructuring agriculture

Agriculture in the Northern Alentejo has to become competitive, in terms of quality and price of its products, vis–à–vis Europe's other farming regions, a need reinforced by Portugal's recent accession to the European Communities. A study is under way to identify produce for which the Alentejo enjoys comparative advantages. Investment for this purpose is being directed towards four interdependent areas: farm infrastructure, farm production, training and information, and agricultural research.

iii) Promoting tourism

The Northern Alentejo is a part of inland Portugal with genuine tourism potential. It still fails to attract sufficient numbers of tourists, who continue to prefer the coast. Given that 20 per cent of holiday arrivals enter Portugal through the Northern Alentejo, the area needs to exploit and enhance its varied tourism resources. The programme includes the development of centres for thermal and sports tourism, and provision of a further 1 200 beds.

iv) Stimulating rural industry

The industrial sector, although relatively small at present, is identified as a major development arena. The programme proposes to encourage new firms, principally in the agro–food sector, high technology and natural resources. Firms will also be supported in efforts to modernise, with technical libraries, training films and economic information.

v) Creating jobs

Developing economic activities helps to create jobs and also retains the rural population, especially younger people. Job creation is one of the programme's targets, and local employment initiatives in both industry and tourism are to be encouraged. The programme will also establish a vocational training system to enhance intersectoral mobility, reduce the dependence on farming and enhance the occupational skills of young people.

THE INTEGRATED DEVELOPMENT OPERATION PARTNERS

A wide array of private and public sector partners, were involved in every stage of the development of the Integrated Development Operation (OID) for the Northern Alentejo. The European Economic Community was an additional major partner, providing technical and financial support. The Community's contribution was decisive in developing the OID, ensuring that the programme was appropriately tailored to the Community's development aims (Objective 5b) and also that specific development initiatives were effectively integrated in the local context.

The partners held discussions and reviews either in working parties or in plenary sessions. Three bodies give formal shape to the partnership: the Monitoring Committee, the Co–ordinating Council and the latter's Standing Committee.

The Monitoring Committee

The Monitoring Committee is made up of representatives of the agencies responsible for establishing the Integrated Development Operation for the Northern Alentejo:

— The Commission of the European Communities;
— The Directorate General for Regional Development;
— The Co–ordinating Commission for the Alentejo region; and
— The local authorities.

The Monitoring Committee meets at least twice a year and is responsible for:

— Co–ordinating selection of OID measures with the administrative and financial partners;
— Co–ordinating measures with OID objectives;
— Co–ordinating publicity relating to the programme;
— Adjusting the programme to economic and social conditions; and
— Reporting annually on the programme.

The Co-ordinating Council

The Co-ordinating Council is made up of representatives of the Agriculture, Forestry, Education and Health Ministries; the Agencies for Employment, Assistance to Enterprise and Tourism promotion; the Highways and Agricultural Engineering directorates; and representatives of local councils, trade unions and associations of employers, farmers and farm workers. The Co-ordinating Council:

— Annually approves proposals to amend the overall programme, in particular any to amend the budget (these require the approval of the Monitoring Committee);
— Supports, monitors and evaluates the execution of the programme; and
— Defines measures needed for proper execution of the programme, and proposes them to the sectors concerned.

The Standing Committee

The Standing Committee of the Co-ordinating Council is made up of the programme administrator and representatives of the:

— Directorate General of Agriculture for the Alentejo;
— Directorate General of Forestry;
— Regional Tourism Committee;
— Support Agency to industrial SMEs; and
— Local councils.

The role of the Committee is to:

— Monitor the execution of the programme on a permanent basis;
— Evaluate progress periodically and report on the impact of the programme;
— Undertake action required for the proper execution of the programme; and
— Organise meetings of the Co-ordinating Council.

PROGRAMME IMPLEMENTATION

Execution and Monitoring

Integrated Development Operation projects are executed in one of two ways:

— directly, by the agency assigned full material and financial responsibility under the programme; and
— under contract, between the agency with financial responsibility under the programme and a body to which a specific project is assigned.

The establishment of a management information system (MIS) ensures rational co-ordination of the material, financial and institutional inputs and of the partnership between investor and beneficiary. This system further assists on-going evaluation and hence allows necessary programme adjustments to be agreed upon and put in place when appropriate. An ex-post evaluation of the OID programme is being prepared, using the methodology developed by the European Commission.

PARTNERSHIPS IN THE INTEGRATED DEVELOPMENT OPERATION FOR THE NORTHERN ALENTEJO (PORTUGAL)

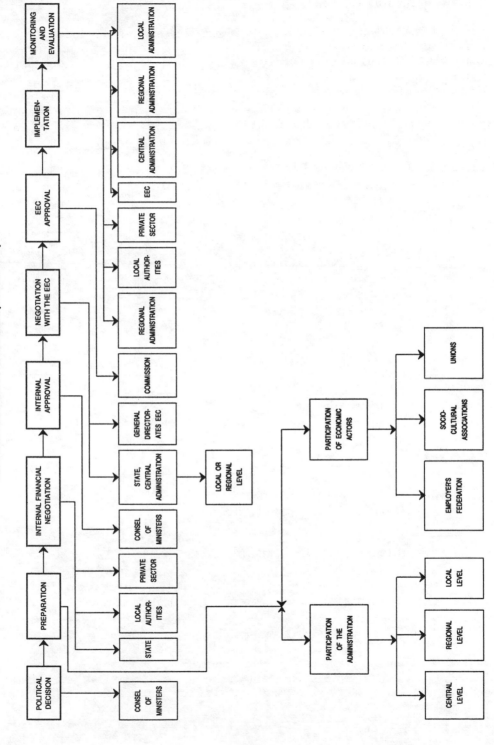

117

SPAIN

SUMMARY

The Mancomunidad of the Lower Guadalquivir is an institutional partnership designed to carry out a local development strategy geared towards job creation and the transformation of an agricultural into an industrial and tertiary economy. It involves intermunicipal co–operation among the nine municipalities of the Lower Guadalquivir region. The Mancomunidad, formed in 1987, is an example of a new type partnership arrangement fostered by the Constitution of 1978 that initiated a process of devolution of authority and responsibility to regions and communities. Evidence to date indicates that the Mancomunidad has the legal and managerial flexibility and political legitimacy to effectively foster local economic development in the Lower Guadalquivir region.

THE MANCOMUNIDAD OF THE LOWER GUADALQUIVIR
A PARTNERSHIP FOR RURAL DEVELOPMENT

The Lower Guadalquivir is formed by a set of nine municipalities in the provinces of Seville and Cadiz. The major productive activities of the region are agriculture, and in the maritime zone, tourism and fishing. Agriculture is the primary economic activity of the region, involving approximately 50 per cent of the active population. The productivity of agriculture is low, and markets for the region's agricultural products are limited. The major challenge of the 1990s for the Lower Guadalquivir is to restructure its economic centre of gravity away from agriculture toward industrial and service sector enterprises competitive in national and international markets.

Two approaches to the region's economic restructuring are possible. One approach is to foster the emigration of labour and local entrepreneurial capacity to developed regions and metropolitan areas where productive activity is already concentrated. Another approach is to design and implement a local development strategy with the objectives of maintaining population and production capacity within the region and of encouraging the immigration of productive capital. The town councils of the municipalities in the Lower Guadalquivir have opted for this latter strategy. They plan to use the Mancomunidad as the agent for the design and implementation of local development policies.

The Mancomunidad of the Lower Guadalquivir is a partnership among the nine municipalities in the region. The formation of this partnership was grounded in four key factors:

— Existence of serious employment and productivity problems in the region;
— Realisation that the solutions to these problems would require joint effort among the nine municipalities;
— Availability of external aid;
— Conviction that the economic problems of the Lower Guadalquivir can best be solved through local collective efforts.

As an inter–municipal partnership for local development, the Mancomunidad of the Lower Guadalquivir is operating within an institutional framework that has undergone important transformations during the last decade. The Constitution of 1978 began a process of devolution of authority and responsibility to regions and local communities. This new reality has opened up the possibility of new types of institutional partnerships among public and among public and private sector actors. The Mancomunidad is an example of such a partnership.

Objectives

The overall purpose of the Mancomunidad of the Lower Guadalquivir is to carry out a local development strategy geared towards job creation and the transformation of an agricultural economy into an industrial and tertiary economy. Specific objectives of the Mancomunidad include:

— Promoting activities to create jobs and to improve the standard of living in the region;
— Fostering change in local economic systems towards activities and enterprises with a comparative advantage in national and international markets;
— Establishing transport and communication infrastructures and services necessary for enhancing local economic development;
— Managing economic and financial aid;
— Coordinating private and public development initiatives and collaborating with agents interested in local development projects.

The Mancomunidad was created for the purpose of promoting development, structural change, and the improvement of the standard of living of the local communities of the region. To achieve this end, the Mancomunidad will try to mobilise human and financial resources, as well as co–ordinate the actions of public and private actors. It is an organisation working on behalf of the local public agents toward implementation of local development strategies in every municipality, which in the future may give way to a common strategy for the entire region.

PARTNERSHIP ORGANISATION AND OPERATION

Direction and Management

The Mancomunidad of the Lower Guadalquiver is a public institution formed by nine municipalities. The agreement creating it, signed by representatives of all the town councils, was submitted and approved by the citizens. The nine town councils are, therefore, local public agents that have associated themselves in the project of promoting and stimulating development in the Lower Guadalquivir.

The direction and management of the Mancomunidad is carried out through three different bodies: the Council of the Mancomunidad, the Government Commission and the President.

— The Council of the Mancomunidad is formed by the mayors of the nine municipalities and other councilmen appointed by every municipality. Its tasks include election of the President and Vice–president of the Council, approval of the budget and all loans above 5 per cent of the total budget, fixing of the amount of the municipality's contributions, and control of the Mancomunidad offices.

— The Government Commission is formed by the President, four vice–presidents and other members of the Council of the Mancomunidad, the latter being elected by the whole Council. It is responsible for the organisation of the services, economic and financial management and contracts for public works and services of the Mancomunidad. Each member of the Government Commission is responsible for one office of the Mancomunidad: tourism, communications and infrastructures, rural roads, culture, training and education, agricultural development, youth and sports, social well–being, and environment.

— The President represents the Mancomunidad, manages the local affairs, stimulates the provision of local services and controls the actions of the Mancomunidad. The President is primary operating officer and oversees use of Mancomunidad resources, services and technical expertise to pursue its objectives.

The Council and the Commission meet periodically (the Council every three months, the Commission every month) as well as on special occasions in order to resolve particular matters. Agreements are reached by simple majority, except for those cases where statutes or the legal norms require a different "quorum". Agreements are legally binding for the municipalities of the Mancomunidad.

The financial resources of the Mancomunidad come primarily from private sources, subsidies and public aid, grants and municipal contributions. A single yearly budget is presented, which must be approved by the Council of the Mancomunidad.

The Mancomunidad is a public body for the co–ordination and management of rural development that receives its competences and power from the municipalities that confer their sovereignty. The Mancomunidad supports the local units and generates scale economies in the administration of services that in turn benefit each of the municipalities.

The Mancomunidad has a short experience to date, and no major conflicts have yet surfaced. Its organisation and functioning, however, generate some contradictions. The decision–making process is affected by the fact that the Mancomunidad is a participatory institution with the substantial power concentrated in the office of the President decentralised among its different offices. The budget (expenditures, and occasionally, revenues), however, must be distributed among the nine municipalities in order to enhance flexibility and effectiveness in addressing locally rural development issues. This budget distribution process forces decisions regarding which areas are the key growth centers in the Lower Guadalquivir region.

Differences in the analysis of problems and the conflict of interests among member municipalities tend to be overcome through discussion in the representative bodies.

The objective is to reach consensus in all decisions. When this is not possible, a vote is taken, and the majority criteria is applied by the President in determining the resolution of an issue. Eventually, when it is not possible to reach an ample majority, a decision is postponed until such a time when a more reflective study of the facts allows for agreement.

The Economic Promotion Office

The Economic Promotion Office is the department through which the Mancomunidad pursues local development policy objectives in the Lower Guadalquivir region. Its primary responsibility is to promote the creation of an environment favourable to developing local and attracting external entrepreneurial activity. The objective is not to foster the free creation and location of firms, but rather to encourage the best investments for each locality by conducting public and private investment projects and by mobilising existing as well as outside investment initiatives.

Creation of the Economic Promotion Office was the inspiration of the President of the Mancomunidad. Its managing director is appointed by the Government Commission. It acts through the central office of the Commission as well as nine delegations, representing each municipality of the Mancomunidad.

The specific functions of the Economic Promotion Office are to provide information and respond to questions regarding development opportunities and initiatives; to consult with rural delegations regarding the coordination and the technical and financial viability of rural projects; to provide training and education to enhance the technical skills of workers and the managerial capacities of local entrepreneurs and managers; and to promote development in the municipalities of the region.

EVALUATION OF THE MANCOMUNIDAD

During its first year, the activity of the Mancomunidad focused mainly on initiating and organising its activities, thus no technical evaluation can be made of its accomplishments. Nevertheless, some strong and weak points of this local development mechanism have emerged.

The Mancomunidad has several significant advantages from the perspective of its municipalities and their town councils. Above all, it is an animating development agent for all the municipalities involved, whose economic actions and projects affect the entire region. The objectives of job creation and improvement of the standard of living can benefit from the scale economies of the Mancomunidad's actions to foster productive restructuring of the regional and local economies and their service delivery systems. Second, the Mancomunidad, thanks to the political strength and legitimacy accorded to it by the collective recognition of all the municipalities, has the capacity to co-ordinate the actions of national, regional and local administrations. Last, the flexibility of the Mancomunidad's legal structure makes it a useful institution for managing and co-ordinating local development policies in the region.

Despite these advantages, the Mancomunidad of the Lower Guadalquivir faces some practical constraints that could limit its efficiency. Above all, it works with a set of diverse municipalities with different production capacities, different levels of development and different experiences with the implementation of local development policy. Furthermore, entrepreneurial capacity in the Lower Guadalquivir region is not well developed, making the task of local public managers in the economic restructuring and adjustment process difficult. Last, the Mancomunidad faces an important lack of human and financial resources to carry out its own role in the economic restructuring of the lower Guadalquivir region.

SWEDEN

SUMMARY

The Rural Policy Advisory Committee was initiated in 1977 with the purpose of improving economic and social conditions in rural Sweden. The Advisory Committee is a partnership among representatives of central and county government, political parties, and several interest groups concerned with rural issues. Since its inception, the Committee has undertaken numerous activities to foster rural development. These activities range from information dissemination and education to initiating and funding rural development projects to providing advice and counsel to government ministries and agencies on rural issues and policy strategies. Through these activities, the Advisory Committee has played a leading catalyst role in the formulation of rural policy. Unlike the numerous other government agencies and organisations concerned with rural issues which represent primarily sectorial or special interests, the Rural Policy Advisory Committee has responsibility for taking an integrated, global approach to rural issues and rural policy.

THE RURAL POLICY ADVISORY COMMITTEE

Loss of population, lack of job opportunities and the decline of amenities, especially in the inland parts of northern Sweden, have for decades necessitated rural policy measures to counter these problems and to strengthen the economic and social vitality of rural areas. Such measures have in fact been taken, with agencies at various levels of government involved in their formulation and implementation. More than ten years ago, the Government appointed a special Rural Policy Advisory Committee to work for improvements in the living conditions of the rural population. The Advisory Committee is a partnership among representatives from the Ministries of Labour and Agriculture, the State County Administrations, the six political parties represented in parliament, and associations representing the interests of municipalities, county councils and farmers. The objectives, the partners and the main activities of the Rural Policy Advisory Committee are described in this summary.

Objectives

The primary objective of the Rural Policy Advisory Committee is to work to improve rural living conditions in various parts of Sweden, but with special emphasis on the more sparsely–populated rural areas of northern inland Sweden, as well as the archipelago communities. The Committee is to consider specific employment problems of rural communities, as well as questions relating to commercial and social services. It shall also consider the co–ordination and intensification of all governmental measures for rural communities.

Historical Background

National government initiatives in the countryside are of long standing in Sweden. The procedures in developing these initiatives have varied from time to time. The first Study Group on Rural Policy was appointed in 1966, and concentrated mainly on questions concerning rural services. Its main concern was to bring about measures of various kinds on the part of national and municipal authorities. At the same time, the Study Group focused on the problems of elderly persons living in rural communities.

The Rural Policy Study Group remained in existence until 1969, when it was succeeded by the Rural Policy Commission. In 1972 this Commission presented a report containing recommendations on commercial services, education, social services, communication and rural employment.

A number of new supportive arrangements were introduced at the beginning of the 1970s. These included an experimental scheme of intensified municipal job creation measures, aimed at providing temporary employment for elderly workers who are unemployed and geographically immobile. At the same time, with a view to securing commodity supplies in rural areas, a subsidisation scheme was introduced for commercial services, comprising investment support and home delivery grants.

A new Rural Policy Study Group was appointed in 1973, this time acting in conjunction with a parliamentary reference group. This new study group concentrated mainly on municipal employment planning and rural service provision issues.

The existing Rural Policy Advisory Committee was set up in 1977. The terms of reference for the Committee's work issued by the Government stated its objectives in broad, general terms and allowed a flexible, wide–ranging working approach commensurate with the scope of the Committee's responsibilities.

COMMITTEE ORGANISATION AND OPERATION

Partners

In 1980 the Rural Policy Advisory Committee acquired a purely parliamentary structure, involving numerous partners representing the national, regional and local levels. At present, the Committee has 60 members. All six parties in the Riksdag have ten representatives on the Committee. It also includes experts representing the Ministries of Labour and Agriculture; the State County Administrations; and three interest organisations, the Federation of Swedish Farmers, the Swedish Association of Local Authorities and the Swedish Federation of County Councils.

As a result of its parliamentary structure, the Committee's recommendations on various questions have a measure of party–political support, which facilitates their progress through the machinery of government and parliament. It should be noted, however, that within the Committee there is a great deal of agreement across party–political boundaries in the discussion of rural affairs, much greater than in the Riksdag, where there is appreciably more emphasis on party divisions. Most of the Committee's decisions are in fact unanimous.

Responsibility for regional and rural policies rested previously with the Ministry of Industry. The Rural Policy Advisory Committee and its operation were initially assigned under the Ministry's jurisdiction as well. On 1st January 1989, however, responsibility for regional and rural policies was transferred to the Ministry of Labour

The Ministries of Labour and Agriculture are integrally involved in Rural Policy Advisory Committee activities. Involvement of the Ministry of Labour is prompted by the importance of rural employment questions, and its overall responsibility for regional and rural policies. Agriculture and forestry are a vital foundation of employment, especially in the rural communities in northern Sweden, hence the involvement of the Ministry of Agriculture.

Rural policy, however, spans a wider range of issues, involving practically all Ministries. Relevant and important issues include, for example, education, communications and the decentralisation of public administration. From time to time, therefore, representatives of other Ministries are also invited to take part in the discussion of questions relating to their responsibilities.

Sweden is divided into 24 counties. Responsibility for the implementation of regional and rural policy is vested in the 24 State County Administrations, which, among other things, decide on the distribution of regional support and rural support, plan and conduct projects of regional importance, and endeavour to co–ordinate sectorial policy.

Agriculture means a great deal to the sparsely populated communities of northern Sweden. In addition to the Ministry of Agriculture, therefore, the farmers' own interest organisation, the Federation of Swedish Farmers, is represented on the Committee.

Municipalities have an important part to play in local development work. Many municipalities have a special enterprise development officer whose responsibility includes rural affairs. The main task of the municipality is to facilitate and encourage the creation of enterprises. Sweden's Local Government Act does not, however, allow municipalities to provide financial support for individual enterprises. Municipal interests are represented on the Committee by the Swedish Association of Local Authorities.

In addition to the State County Administrations, there are also county councils in Sweden. These councils, like the municipal councils, are elected bodies with independent powers of taxation. They are above all responsible for health care and medical services, an important service problem in rural areas due to the relatively large percentage of elderly persons living in these areas, long distances to caring amenities and, sometimes, a diminishing population base for the maintenance of adequate services. In some county council areas, there has recently been a growth of council interest in questions of industrial and regional policy. County councils are represented on the Advisory Committee by their own national organisation, the Swedish Federation of County Councils.

Committee Activities

Like its predecessors, the Rural Policy Advisory Committee devoted a great deal of time during its initial years to analysing the problems and development potential of rural communities. Previous committees, however, had concentrated almost entirely on ways of relieving or solving specific rural problems. The Advisory Committee began instead to identify the many advantages and resources of rural communities and areas which could be utilised in fostering rural development. This new approach, which has received increasing attention during the past decade, has imparted a more proactive, offensive character to rural policy, grounded in a positive view of rural resources and opportunities.

The Advisory Committee is also involved in rural policy and programme formulation. An important task during its initial phase was to help other authorities design measures to support development in rural areas, and this work is continuing today. Also, the Advisory Committee, acting either independently or together with other authorities, frequently carries out investigations resulting in recommendations for the amendment of current rules and legislation.

The Advisory Committee was allotted limited funds during its early years, primarily for research activities. The annual budget was less than SKr 1 million. During the early 1980s, the Committee was also allotted a limited amount of project funding, to be applied to experimental activities and participation in pilot projects for rural development. This funding has gradually been augmented, and for the past two fiscal years the Committee's budget has balanced at a total of SKr 5 million.

Despite this increased funding, the Committee's project activities have, financially, been entirely dependent on co-funding. Most often, the Committee's own financial contribution to a project is very slight compared with the contributions made by municipalities, State County Administrations and other interested parties. The Committee has committed the bulk of its resources during the 1980s to projects focusing on local development, new technology, education and research, agriculture and forestry, sectorial co-operation and dual employment. The aim has been to select pilot projects of strategic importance which can open the way to future changes in attitudes or regulations.

Many projects have been completed or are currently underway. The following two examples illustrate the nature and scope of the Committee's project work. In three municipalities, the Committee has initiated a "village of the future" project. This initiative is an attempt to facilitate positive developments in a number of villages, based on concerted measures to investigate the possibility of the traditional village not only surviving but also becoming an attractive alternative to modern towns. The Committee has also long been working to extend the benefits of new information technology to rural communities by developing "telecommunications cottages". The basic principle underlying this effort is that many of the tasks now being done in towns and cities with the aid of modern telecommunications can equally well be done in the countryside. The Committee has collaborated with the National Telecommunications Administration, among other bodies, in setting up a large number of "telecommunications cottages". Before long, there will be about 40 such centres in various parts of the country, with computers, telex, telefax and other modern equipment.

Through its participation in a host of such projects, both large and small, the Committee's Secretariat has built up an extensive network of contacts throughout the country. This network includes municipalities, State County Administrations, researchers, organisations, national administrative boards and decisionmakers at various levels. In recent years, this network has expanded, as a result of the Committee's responsibility for co–ordinating Sweden's participation in the Campaign for the Countryside launched by the Council of Europe.

The Committee's extensive network of contacts built up over the years can be used by its Secretariat to influence discussions, decisions and policy initiatives related to rural areas. Since the Committee Chairman represents the largest Riksdag party and, accordingly, the Government as well, viewpoints on rural policy can be conveyed to the Government and Riksdag through informal political channels. Similarly, other Committee members from various political parties can pursue questions of rural policy within their respective party organisations.

Sectorial co–operation among national authorities is often a matter of attitude changes and determination to explore new, unconventional forms of co–operation. In this respect, the Committee has often played a catalyst role in bringing various organisations and interests together. Its limited project funds can sometimes be applied to a pilot study leading to more concrete joint projects in which the relevant authorities themselves eventually take charge.

One of the Committee's important tasks is to disseminate knowledge of current rural policy issues and policy initiatives. The Committee carries out this task by issuing its own publications or taking part in the production of publications by other bodies; providing information to news media regarding discussions at Committee meetings; answering a large number of inquiries about rural development from the general public, national authorities and organisations; and by taking part in and sometimes arranging conferences and seminars on rural affairs.

TURKEY

SUMMARY

The "Sanliurfa–Ceylanpinar iki Circip Sprinkler Irrigation Project" focuses on one of the least developed regions of Turkey. This project involves partnerships among four different agencies associated with three different national ministries. Through regular communication, problems of inter–agency co–ordination have been anticipated and resolved. This project demonstrates that integrated development initiatives, grounded in effective organisation and management, can lead to more efficient use of resources and accelerated development in under-developed regions. The project has resulted in increased local investment, improved agricutural productivity and creation of additional employment opportunities. Agricultural production for market instead of family consumption is one of the project's the most extraordinary results. This transformation is important in integrating the economy of the project area with the national economy and society.

THE SANLIURFA–CEYLANPINAR IKI CIRCIP
SPRINKLER IRRIGATION PROJECT

Rural development policy in Turkey is aimed at fully integrating rural areas into the national economy. Rapid industrialisation, however, is increasing the gap in living standards between rural and non–rural areas. Change in the structure of agriculture and the transformation to a more diversified economy are regarded as important first steps in the rural development process. Since the beginning of the Turkish Republic, numerous rural development policies have been implemented and substantial resources have been directed toward improving the social and economic viability of rural areas. Based on this considerable experience, the principles of integrated development planning have for some time provided a framework for guiding the formulation and implementation of Turkish rural development policy. The Sanliurfa–Ceylanpinar iki Circip Sprinkler Irrigation Project, implemented through a partnership of several key governmental agencies, illustrates the application of this integrated perspective.

131

Objectives

The Sanliurfa–Ceylanpinar iki Circip Sprinkler Irrigation Project is a small part of the larger Southeastern Anatolia Project. When the sprinkler irrigation project was initiated in 1975, its purpose was to accelerate the region's socio–economic development by establishing irrigated agriculture, utilising the plentiful supply of underground water available in the region. As the project evolved, however, it incorporated other initiatives aimed at improving infrastructure, thus becoming an integrated project.

The Project Area

The project, which encompasses 207 km², is in Southeast Turkey, at the east of Urfa Province where Atatürk Dam and Urfa Tunnel are located, and at the point where Urfa and Mardin Provinces and Syria intersect. The amount of land suitable for agriculture totals 15 000 ha: 11 000 ha belong to the State and 4 000 ha belong to private farmers. According to the results of the 1975 census, 5 780 people live in the project area. The birth rate is 3.8 per cent, and the population density is 59 persons/km².

The project area includes fifty–five settlement units or hamlets. These units are quite separate from each other. In an administrative sense, they are attached to one administrative unit, or Muhtarlik, namely Muratli. This Muhtarlik is attached to the town of Ceylanpinar. The settlement units in the project area are located between 7 and 27 km from Ceylanpinar.

Before the project started, public services and facilities were limited. Primary schools existed in three settlement units, a health house in one. A soil–water research station was also located in the project area. Families used the health services and education facilities existing in neighbouring villages or in Ceylanpinar. None of the settlement units had running tap water systems, electricity or modern communication systems. Water was provided from wells 75–80 m deep by mechanical power. The roads in the area were in poor condition, their quality not meeting minimum standards. Access to the settlement units was difficult during winter.

Social and economic development in the project area accelerated after 1950, paralleling the development trend in the nation as a whole. Up until the 1950s, the area was primarily pasture owned by the State, with livestock holders living there only for their winter stay. As time passed, some families became involved with more diverse agricultural enterprises. In 1952, the State passed a law distributing a certain part of the area to landless nomad families, and landless farmers began to congregate in permanent settlements. Substantial nomadic migration continued into the 1970s, however.

In the early 1970s, the Ministry of Rural Affairs and Co–operatives initiated research and planning efforts designed to solve the area's economic and demographic problems. Surveys showed that fallow dryland farming and livestock (sheep and goats) were the main agricultural enterprises of the area. Many farmers cultivated rented land from the State. Families without land or animal husbandry activities made their livings as agricultural workers.

PROJECT IMPLEMENTATION

Partners

Four different agencies attached to three different ministries have been involved in implementing the project.

— The Undersecretariat of Land and Agriculture Reform in the Ministry of Agriculture, Forestry and Rural Affairs provides financial support, is responsible for distributing land by the end of the project, and supports agricultural establishments by creating co–operatives.

— The General Directorate of State Hydraulic Works is responsible for drilling exploratory wells, setting vertical and horizontal pumps, and establishing electrical boards.

— The General Directorate of Land and Water in the Ministry of Agriculture, Forestry and Rural Affairs plans the closed–circuit distribution of water, provides equipment necessary for sprinkler irrigation, and constructs roads necessary for the application of the project.

— The Turkish Electricity Authority in the Ministry of Energy and Natural Resources installs transformers and transformer–board connections necessary to draw electricity from the national electricity distribution system.

The responsibilities of these different agencies were clearly indicated in the project protocol. According to this protocol, electricity would be brought to the project area, exploratory wells would be drilled, farm irrigation equipment would be supplied, closed water circuits installed, field parcelisation and road networks necessary for irrigation established and agricultural co–operatives organised.

Co–operation and Co–ordination

At the beginning of the project, co–operation and co–ordination among the agencies involved was well established, so there was no need for a new organisation or authority. The agencies were expected to fulfill their responsibilities as a part of their yearly investment programmes through their regional or provincial directorates.

Since the beginning, the operation of the project has been evaluated every six months by the senior directors of the responsible agencies or their representatives and local governors. In these meetings, the work completed has been discussed and new study programmes have been elaborated. In addition, existing and anticipated inter-agency co–operation and co–ordination problems have been discussed and resolved.

PROJECT IMPACT

In the project area, the land suitable for agriculture is 15 244 ha On 9 000 ha of this land, irrigated agriculture has been established as a consequence of the project. The irrigated land includes 7 503 ha belonging to the State, and 2 675 ha owned by farmers. Of the non–irrigated land, 3 454 ha are owned by the State and 1 596 ha by farmers. Some of the land which is owned by the State is rented by the farmers. Families involved in the intensive irrigated agriculture in the project area will be good examples for the other farmers when the Southeast Anatolian Project is completed because of the experience they are gaining with this type of agriculture.

Agricultural productivity has improvd rapidly as a result of the project. The vegetable production requirement of the region, for example, was met by the neighbouring provinces before the implementation of the project. But now, there is a surplus of vegetables, allowing producers to respond to the market demand for fresh vegetables in neighbouring provinces.

The development of public services and facilites has also accelerated as a result of the project. Twenty–six settlement units have been provided with primary schools, forty–five with electricity, and forty–six with roads. The need for running tap water in the area is met, to some extent, by the irrigation water system. Additional capacity is required, however. The General Directorate of Rural Services is working to establish a tap water distribution system that will meet this need.

Two ministries and their attached agencies were primarily responsible for the delivery of rural services until 1985. Some other ministries, such as Health, Energy and Natural Resources, and National Education, were also involved. After 1985, the two primary Ministries, the Ministry of Rural Affairs and Co–operatives and the Ministry of Agriculture and Forestry, were integrated to form the Ministry of Agriculture, Forestry and Rural Affairs. The development of villages, agriculture and forestry is now the responsibility of this Ministry.

UNITED KINGDOM

SUMMARY

The Rural Development Commission is the principal agency for carrying forward the Government's rural development policies and programmes in England. The Commission works in partnership with a wide range of governmental, community, and private sector agencies and organisations in pursuing this goal. The Rural Development Commission is one example among the many institutional partnerships involving central government departments and agencies, local governments, private sector enterprises and community voluntary organisations for implementing rural policies and programmes in the United Kingdom.

PARTNERSHIPS FOR RURAL POLICY IMPLEMENTATION IN THE UK

The Government of the United Kingdom has developed a package of policies designed to smooth the path of change in the countryside and to create a framework within which the vital objectives of a healthy rural economy and an attractive rural environment can be achieved. A large number of government departments and other public and private sector organisations work as partners to carry forward these policies. This summary details the main types of partnerships for the implementation of rural policies and describes, as an example, the operation of a government–sponsored body, the Rural Development Commission.

Central Government Departments

Central government departments co–operate to ensure that they develop compatible policies for rural areas and that the means exist for implementing those policies. For example, the Government's Farming and Rural Enterprise policy package which was issued on 10th March 1987 described the Government's policies on agriculture and rural enterprise and development, and explained what the Government and its

135

agencies were doing to carry those policies forward. Government departments co-operated in the preparation of this package, which was launched jointly the by the Secretary of State for the Environment, the Minister of Agriculture, Fisheries and Food, and the Secretaries of State for Wales, Nothern Ireland and Scotland. In July 1988 the same government departments got together to set out the Government's policy towards the environment and to explain who is reponsible for what in environmental protection, including the protection of the countryside.

Central government also works in close co-operation with other organisations to see that its policies for rural areas are carried forward effectively and efficiently. Some regulation is needed, as in the case of land use planning, but the Government's main task is to guide and encourage. Advice is issued to organisations involved in the implementation of rural policies and, where appropriate, funds are made available.

Government Agencies

Much of the work in implementing the Government's rural policies is carried out by specialist agencies funded largely from government resources. The principal agencies concerned with the protection of the countryside are the two Countryside Commissions (one for England and Wales, one for Scotland), the Nature Conservancy Council and the Department of the Environment for Northern Ireland. The Rural Development Commission is the principal agency in England responsible for carrying forward the Government's proposals for diversifying rural enterprise.

The Countryside Commissions have particular responsibility for conserving the landscape and promoting recreation in the countryside. They advise the Government on landscape conservation and recreation; have responsibility for the designation of protected areas such as National Parks in England and Wales and National Scenic Areas in Scotland; and provide grants for long-distance routes, country parks tree planting, and other conservation work.

The Nature Conservancy Council advises the Government and others on nature conservation; establishes and manages National Nature Reserves and designates Sites of Special Scientific Interest; and conducts research and disseminates knowledge on nature conservation.

In England the Rural Development Commission is responsible for implementing the Government's rural enterprise diversification programmes. In Wales the task is undertaken primarily by the Development Board for Rural Wales, known as Mid Wales Development and the Welsh Development Agency. In Scotland the Scottish Development Agency and the Highlands and Islands Development Board fulfil similar functions.

The Government works closely with each of these agencies in the development of their strategies for the future and in the preparation of programmes of future work known as Corporate Plans. Preparing and rolling forward these plans enables the agencies to develop and justify strategies and programmes for the future which are clearly linked to rural needs and problems, relevant government policies and the likely availability of resources.

All of the government agencies also work in co-operation with one another and with a range of other public and private agencies with an interest in the countryside. For example, the Nature Conservancy Council has a "Partnership in Practice" initiative. Its purpose is to promote collaborative working relationships resulting in better awareness of nature conservation requirements, more understanding of the problems faced by the productive sector, and a climate of mutual trust within which nature conservation can be integrated effectively into the policies and practices of others.

The Private Sector

The Government wishes to see greater private sector involvement in rural areas. It is anxious to encourage local enterprise and to minimise public sector involvement wherever possible. With this objective in mind, the Government has entered into partnerships with the private sector in several areas. For example, both the private sector and Central Government provide funds for Local Enterprise Agencies. These agencies cover many rural areas, providing a range of support services to small businesses, which may include advice and counselling, workshop provision and training.

A number of government agencies have also developed partnership schemes which are intended to stimulate private sector activity in rural areas. For example, the Scottish Development Agency has a scheme called PRIDE which offers grants and loans to projects which create employment or improve the rural environment, with the proviso that the greater part of any project costs must be met by the private sector. In England and Wales, broadly similar experimental schemes known as ACCORD and DRIVE were launched in 1987 and 1986. Both experiments are being revised before decisons are taken on continuing them in the future.

Local Government

Local authorities have an important role to play in making and implementing rural policy. Not only are they land use planning authorities, but they also provide services in rural areas, promote rural economic and social development and make a major contribution to nature conservation.

In Great Britain local authorities have operated a comprehensive Town and Country planning system for more than forty years. Acting within the requirements of legislation and government policy, they draw up plans which provide a framework for development and decide whether permission should be given for new buildings or other development. In this way, local authorities are able to carry forward the Government's policies on rural areas by striking the right balance between the needs of development and the interests of conservation.

Many local authorities also carry forward the Government's policies for rural areas by encouraging economic development in rural areas which have problems. As the authorities are in close touch with local problems and local organisations, they are often in a good position to get new ideas off the ground and to help voluntary bodies and private enterprise tackle problems.

A number of authorities have also made major contributions to nature conservation by providing for it in their policy–making and by supporting specific projects. For example, some authorities have appointed specialist advisors to work with appropriate professional institutions and voluntary bodies, and some have established statutory Local Nature Reserves.

Voluntary Organisations

Voluntary organisations play a valuable part in carrying forward the Government's policies for rural areas. Many voluntary organisations take a lively interest in the protection of the countryside and nature conservation. Some have developed a wide range of expertise and provide a valuable source of advice for local authorities as well as taking an active role in environmental protection. Such organisations range from small local groups concerned about the conservation of local amenities to large national organisations. For example, the National Trust for Scotland makes many of the nation's outstanding historic buildings and much attractive countryside available to visitors. The Royal Society for the Protection of Birds and the Royal Society for Nature Conservation, together with the county–based naturalists trusts, have had a profound influence on nature conservation throughout this century. In fact, most of Britain's nature reserves are run by voluntary bodies.

Voluntary organisations also help to encourage rural economic and social development. There are many examples of people in rural areas forming groups or co–operatives to further rural enterprise. Voluntary organisations can also help rural communities to analyse their problems and find a way forward. For example, they can help to deliver services, provide advice, encourage enterprise and provide a link between governmental authorities and the rural community.

THE RURAL DEVELOPMENT COMMISSION

The experiences of the Rural Development Commission, which is the Government's principal agency for the economic and social development of rural areas in England, provide good examples of partnerships among a wide range of agencies and individuals in both public and private sectors. The history, role and organisation and operation of the Commission and some examples of partnerships in which the Commission is involved are described in this section.

History

The history of the Rural Development Commission goes back to 1909 when Development Commissioners were appointed to consider and make recommendations on applications for advances from a Development Fund for rural areas administered by Central Government. This arrangement continued until 1984, when new legislation set up the Development Commission as a government–financed agency fully accountable for its own expenditure.

In April 1988 the Development Commission merged with its main agency, the Council for Small Industries in Rural Areas (CoSIRA), to form the Rural Development Commission. The merger has allowed the Commission to provide a more effective service and to develop a more flexible organisation better able to respond to the diverse and changing circumstances in rural areas. The Commission, which is sponsored by the Department of the Environment, employs about 350 full–time staff and about 100 private sector consultants. It spends about £34 million a year.

Role

The Rural Development Commission has a statutory duty to advise Central Government on matters affecting rural areas. It is also able to carry out, or help others to carry out, measures likely to further the economic and social development of rural England. In order to make the best use of its limited resources, the Commission concentrates its activities in areas of greatest need. These areas, known as Rural Development Areas, were defined in 1984 and cover 35 per cent of England.

In addition to its advisory role, the Commission works in two main fields. It provides support for rural enterprise and helps with the development of rural communities.

Under its economic programmes, the Commission helps firms to set up or expand in rural areas by assisting them with premises, advice, finance and training. The Government wishes to see premises for rural firms provided by the private sector. However, in some areas the return on investment is too low to attract private sector investment and the Commission has a building programme for workshops in the Rural Development Areas. The workshops may be leased or sold to the small firms that occupy the buildings. Sites are also made available for private sector development and the Commission develops sites in partnership with local authorities. Within the Rural Development Areas it also offers grants for small-scale conversions of redundant buildings.

To help small businesses grow, the Commission provides a wide range of advice, financial help and training. A network of local offices supported by private–sector–led local committees is able to provide general advice, supported where necessary by expert advice on management, marketing and technical matters. The Commission assists small businesses to raise finance from banks and other institutions where possible, and has its own loan fund which can be used to supplement the finance available from elsewhere. Grants are also available for marketing and for projects, usually in the Rural Development Areas, that will contribute towards enterprise and the creation of jobs.

The Rural Development Commission aims to ensure that rural services are maintained and, where possible, improved. It has schemes to help provide village halls and other community facilities, and it operates a special fund, financed by the Department of Transport, to encourage innovative transport projects. In other cases, the Commission has no direct role in providing services, but works to influence decisionmakers and suggests possible solutions by showing the way through experimental schemes.

Organisation and Operation

The basis of the Commission is set out in legislation specifying its responsibilities, powers and administrative arrangements. The legislation provides for up to 12 Members of the Rural Development Commission, to be appointed by the Queen. The Commission is supported by staff headed by a chief officer appointed with the approval of the Secretary of State, who is the leading Minister in the Department of the Environment.

The Commission and the Department of the Environment work closely together on the preparation of the Commission's annual corporate plan and on monitoring and evaluating its performance.

For each of the last four years, the Rural Development Commission has produced a corporate plan, setting out its objectives, reporting on progress in meeting them, and describing strategies for the future. Preparation of the plan provides a valuable mechanism for discussing future directions for Commission programmes at a time when the countryside is undergoing radical change and public funds are limited. The plans enable Ministers to assess the Commission's proposed activities and their effectiveness and to reach decisions on the funding level. They also provide an important tool for the Commission's management by setting out objectives for staff and by providing others with a clear idea of the agency's priorities for the future.

The Department of the Environment and the Commission are also working together to improve the peformance monitoring and measurement of Commission activities used to ensure that they provide good value for money. The Commission produces a series of performance indicators every six months recording what has been achieved on each of their programmes. In conjunction with the Department, it has also developed a number of targets to aim for: for example, a target rate of return on the money invested in its factory building programme. The Department and the Commission are working together to improve these indicators and targets and, in particular, to relate the achievements of each programme to the money spent on it.

Partnerships between the Rural Development Commission and Others

In order to meet its objectives and to promote a strategic approach to rural development, the Rural Development Commission works in partnerships with the private sector and a wide range of government departments and agencies. These partnerships take a variety of forms and fulfil a wide range of functions. The Commission may:

— Act as the primary agent in carrying forward central government policies;
— Encourage others to form partnerships in order to pool knowledge and experience to improve conditions;
— Act in co–equal partnership with other agencies; and
— Provide funds for the private sector or local authorities for developments which will lead to additional employment and encourage private sector enterprise.

The following examples are illustrative of these different types of partnerships.

— Since 1st April 1986 the Department of Transport has made available to the Rural Development Commission £1 million in special funding each year to encourage the provision of innovative transport projects to serve the needs of people living in rural areas. The Commission has used the funds to provide grants for projects such as new taxi bus and minibus services, multi–purpose vehicles and car–sharing schemes. It also provides a Rural Transport Advisory Service and funds projects which will give more general benefits to rural communities, for example by providing information.
— Since 1985/86, the Commission has encouraged local authorities and others with an interest in the countryside to come together to assess the problems, needs and potentials of the Commission's priority Rural Development Areas and to draw up rural development programmes to address them. These programmes stimulate and promote contact and co–operation among the agencies and organisations involved and enable the Commission to receive and assess applications for assistance and to seek to lever and input from others.

140

— The Commission's major partners in promoting community development activity are the Rural Community Councils (RCCs). The RCCs are county–wide voluntary organisations which represent community needs and promote community development. The Commission provides financial support for the administrative costs and community development work of the Councils and encourages local initiatives with grants payable through the RCCs.

— In July 1987 the Commission launched ACCORD, an 18–month experimental scheme aimed at helping private companies and individuals overcome some of the commercial problems of running a profitable business in the countryside. Key purposes of this scheme are to encourage new commercial activities that will lead to additional employment and to revitalise and strengthen the rural economy by encouraging increased private sector investment and helping new businesses to get off the ground.

CONCLUSIONS

Implementation of the Government's rural policies involves partnerships with a very wide range of organisations and individuals. Examination of a sample of the activities of just one of the organisations working in partnership with the Government, the Rural Development Commission, reveals partnerships with central and local government, the private sector and a wide array of voluntary organisations.

The involvement of such a broad range of bodies means that particular care has to be taken to ensure that functions are not duplicated and that overlaps are minimized. In addition, care has to be taken to ensure that clients do not become confused about which agency to approach. To keep these problems in check, close liaison among those involved is necessary, together with carefully considered objectives, clear business or corporate plans and monitoring. Review of individual schemes, agencies or groups of agencies, in the light of changes in circumstances or government policy, can also help to identify gaps or overlaps in activity and to suggest improvements for the future.

Despite the close co–operation and co–ordination required, such wide–ranging partnership arrangements have many advantages. They help to ensure that available skills and abilities are used to the best advantage, and that knowledge of local circumstances is put to good use and reflected in national programmes of assistance. Most importantly, the involvement of the private sector and local interest groups helps to encourage private sector development and local enterprise and reduce the need for public sector intervention.

UNITED STATES

SUMMARY

Rural areas in Georgia have been able to effectively address their cyclical and structural unemployment problems through the Job Training Partnership Act. This Act is grounded in a complex matrix of partnership relationships among federal, state and local governments and among government and private sector actors. Much of the responsibility for implementation of the JTPA rests with a partnership of public and private actors at a local sub–state level, with the private sector partners playing a significant role in the partnership. The JTPA is designed to provide job training for economically disadvantaged and dislocated workers. Its organisation and operation are based on the decentralisation of governmental authority for job training from the federal to state and local governments, a central feature of current federal job training policy in the United States.

THE JOB TRAINING PARTNERSHIP ACT

In the United States, most workers are trained without government involvement, but since the 1950s the federal government has provided funds for job training programmes. Decentralisation or devolution of federal authority for job training to state and local governments is an important central feature of current federal job–training policy. The current federal legislation for training workers, the Job Training Partnership Act (JTPA), mandates the participation of three levels of government — federal, state and local — and both the public and private sectors. This summary details the objectives and key features of the Job Training Partnership Act, outlines its organisation and operation and describes its implementation in rural areas in the state of Georgia.

Objectives

Displacement of workers by automation was the perceived problem addressed by federal government training policy in the 1950s and early 1960s. In the mid–1960s, in

143

the wake of the civil rights movement and President Lyndon Johnson's War on Poverty, this focus was replaced by a new emphasis on training the economically disadvantaged. Since that time, job training assistance for the economically disadvantaged has remained the primary objective of federal job training policy.

Key Features

Decentralisation of federal job training programme decisions began with the Comprehensive Employment and Training Act (CETA) of 1973. Distribution of CETA funds was made on a "revenue–sharing" basis in which designated local and state governments received a fair share distribution of funds based on the proportions of poor and unemployed people living within their jurisdictions. Implicit in the new decentralisation was the idea that local government can best recognise local labour market problems and can best choose appropriate training programmes. Nevertheless, federal government agencies monitored CETA–funded efforts closely and provided considerable advice.

The replacement of CETA by JTPA in 1982 introduced three significant new features. First, private sector employers were to be brought into federally–supported job training as major participants. Second, although JTPA continued the emphasis on serving the economically disadvantaged population, it added a new group to be assisted: "dislocated workers". Dislocated workers were defined as those whose jobs have disappeared because of structural transformations including plant closings, relocations and exportation of jobs abroad, all important problems in the late 1970s and 1980s. The third significant new feature of JTPA was a broadening of the role of the 50 states.

PROGRAMME IMPLEMENTATION

Involvement and Roles of Different Levels of Government

Administration of JTPA has proceeded from three underlying ideas. First, there is great diversity of economic conditions and consequently of job training needs among the 50 states and among the many thousands of localities within these states. Second, within broad guidelines established at the national level, each state should determine the structure of the programme within its own boundaries. Third, programmes at the local service delivery level should be managed by governmental units that can respond to local job training needs most effectively.

The intended roles of federal, state and local government in JTPA followed directly from these assumptions. At the national level (US Congress and federal government administration), the legislative initiative for JTPA was taken in 1982. The federal government continues to control the broad outline of the programme through annual appropriations for the programme segments, and by amendment of the legislation. At the state level, the structure of the programme within each state was established in the first year through delineation of sub–state service areas and through

144

negotiations with officials of local government units. State governments are also able to retain state level control of certain specified portions of the programme if they so choose, and they review local service delivery plans. At the sub–state or local service delivery level, programme officials exercise direct control over the largest segments of the programme: job training services to economically disadvantaged persons as well as a large portion of the services provided to dislocated workers. Also, it is at the local service delivery level that private sector employers are empowered to exercise their strongest influence in shaping job training programmes.

Within these broad outlines, JTPA legislation allows considerable latitude to states in working out the exact balance of state–level *versus* local control of the programmes. In fact, there has been considerable diversity among states in the working–out of these relationships, but three distinct patterns have emerged. In some states, Governors, the state chief executive officers, took an active role in shaping the programme and re- formed the employment/training systems in their states, forging new "partnerships" at the sub–state level in the process. In other states, Governors took an active role in order to accomplish specific policy goals (such as establishing new statewide economic development programmes), but essentially missed the opportunity to form new partner- ships with localities. In a third group of states, the organisational status quo existing under previous job training programmes continued and no new partnerships were formed.

Organisation and Operation

The federal government has given substantial authority over the JTPA programme to the states. The JTPA legislation specifies within broad limits the administrative structure for achieving shared state/local programme authority, but wide latitude is given to the 50 states and thousands of units of local government as to how they actu- ally organise administratively to operate the programme.

State Partners

Federal law required the Governors of each state to establish a State Job Training Co–ordinating Council, one–third of the members of which must represent private sector employers, to advise the Governor on job training needs in the state, to organise state–level administration of JTPA and to recommend how the state was to be divided geographically into local "service delivery areas" (SDAs).

Congress also intended that each state should co–ordinate the activities of the various state agencies which perform functions related to job training such as voca- tional education, employment placement, rehabilitation services, public assistance, provision of special services to older workers, etc. Since these other agencies typically maintain local or sub–state regional offices, the congressional requirement for co–ordi- nation has meant that they must necessarily become involved with local or regional agencies delivering JTPA services. In this way, JTPA has required creation of a "part- nership" of state, regional and local agencies which might not otherwise work together in concert.

Local Service Delivery Areas

For the purpose of organising local administration of JTPA, the most important state–level activity in each state was drawing the lines to cover the entire state geographically with SDAs. In practice, two alternate ways of delineating SDAs developed, both permitted under the federal law. In the "top–down" method, state officials and Governors proposed SDA boundaries that would conform to divisions of the state that had existed previously for other state activities, thus rationalising sub–state regions. In the "bottom–up" method, cities or combinations of local government units which had previous administrative experience in employment and training programmes sought to retain that status by requesting SDA designation from the state.

In less populous rural states, the "top–down" method of SDA designation prevailed. Governors in those states did not have to respond to designation requests from large local jurisdictions and instead promoted SDA designations according to a state–determined plan. Usually these plans correspond to a pre–existing scheme for combining the counties of the state into a number of economic development districts. In spite of attempts to minimise the total number of SDAs created, approximately 600 SDAs, varying greatly in area and population, were established among the 50 states.

Local Partners

The JTPA legislation requires participation at the SDA level from several major "actors", including local elected officials in the area, a Private Industry Council (PIC) and an administrative agency. The act allows great flexibility in terms of which local agencies and officials perform the designated roles; only the composition of the PIC is fixed by the law: a majority of its members must represent privately–owned businesses. The PICs, with the concurrence of the elected officials, determine the choice of an administrative agency to operate the programme. Possible administrative agencies included local offices of state agencies, local government agencies, local community colleges, vocational or technical schools, local Chambers of Commerce and regional economic development agencies, among others. In many SDAs, elected officials retreated from the foreground and became subsidiary to the Private Industry Councils once an agency had been selected to administer the JTPA programme. This tended to occur where there were numerous small units of local government within one SDA, as is the case in many rural areas.

Given relative freedom in which to operate, some PICs have taken a dominant role in setting local JTPA policy, practising stringent review of actions taken by programme administrators. Other PICs have chosen to function in a "co–equal" relationship with programme administrators. Still other PICs advise only, or react to initiatives from programme staff or local elected officials. The difference in patterns of PIC involvement at the SDA level underscore the flexibility inherent in the JTPA legislation.

Funding

More than one–half of funds allocated by Congress to the states for JTPA are passed through to the local SDAs, but, at both the federal and state levels, some funds are retained for special programmes. Congress allocated funds separately for the "economically disadvantaged" and "dislocated worker" segments in JTPA. 78 per cent of each state's total federal allocation in the economically disadvantaged programme segment must be passed on by the state to its local SDAs. In the recently-revised dislocated worker programme segment, 50 per cent of each state's federal allocation must be distributed to the local SDAs. This change represents a gain for local SDAs relative to states which have controlled all dislocated worker programme funds until mid-1989. Total state-level control of dislocated worker funds led to a bias against small and rural SDAs in some states. Even though a major portion of the programme funds are distributed to the SDAs, each state must review the service plans of its SDAs for adherence to the federal JTPA statute and regulations and for adherence to any additional state policies or regulations governing JTPA.

JTPA IN RURAL GEORGIA

Organising JTPA in Georgia was a challenge since the state is a geographically large area divided into 159 counties. Most Georgia counties are rural and sparsely populated, and each has its own elected officials. Potential actors in job training service delivery at the sub-state SDA level include regional offices of various state agencies, vocational-technical schools, community colleges, non-profit community-based organisations and county and municipal governments. Except in metropolitan areas, governmental units in Georgia tend to be too small and inexperienced to administer a complex grant programme such as JTPA.

Even in the rural areas of Georgia, however, local service delivery in the private-sector-oriented JTPA programme has been successful. The Northeast Georgia SDA provides one example of effective co-operation among governmental units and agencies and between the public and private sectors through the JTPA.

Comprising ten counties, one of which is populous and contains the state university, the Northeast Georgia SDA nevertheless can be charcterised as a predominantly rural area. Textile, apparel, wood products and plastic manufacturing are economically important industries, and employment in services is also significant. Many of the economically disadvantaged population receive public assistance. The closing of obsolescent factories, particularly textile mills, has dislocated many of the area's workers. Hence the job training programme is challenged to prepare both the structurally and cyclically unemployed for new jobs.

In determining the composition of the Private Industry Council for Northeast Georgia, the local elected officials made sure that each of the ten counties was represented by at least one private sector member. Other representatives on the PIC included personnel from the area offices of state agencies. In this way, local co-ordination of job training could be integrated with related services funded by state and/or federal funds.

The Northeast Georgia PIC has been active and assertive in setting policy, monitoring and evaluating programme administration. The PIC and its administrative agency do not operate job training services directly. Instead, local job training programmes are sub-contracted to other organisations, making the selection of contractors the PIC's most important decision.

The state government provided technical assistance on problems associated with sub–contracting and other issues during the first two years of JTPA. This technical assistance from the state was crucial to the Northeast Georgia and other rural SDAs which were new to job training education and to administration of complex grant programmes.

COMMISSION OF THE EUROPEAN COMMUNITIES

PARTNERSHIP FOR RURAL DEVELOPMENT AND THE REFORM OF THE EUROPEAN COMMUNITY'S STRUCTURAL FUNDS

The Treaty of Rome, which is the European Economic Community's basis in law, was recently amended, fundamentally, by the Single European Act, whose entry into force set new targets for the Community together with an appropriate legal framework within which to achieve them.

One such target is to strengthen the Community's socio–economic cohesion, which has been somewhat strained both by the recent enlargement and also by natural tendencies for internal disparities to widen.

Full achievement of this target also calls for suitable financial resources and it is precisely to make these available that the Structural Funds[1], the Community's financial resources earmarked for structural adjustment, are being reformed so that they can be more effectively marshalled and deployed.

The reform will have the effect of doubling these funds from their 1987 level by 1993. Between 1988 and 1993, the Commission will be devoting over Ecus 60 billion to structural projects. The 1989 budget of Ecus 9 billion for the three funds will have risen to Ecus 15 billion in 1993 (see table at the end of the chapter).

Reform of the structural funds is based on five principles:

— Concentration of funding;
— Partnership;
— Coherence with national economic policies;
— Better management;
— Simplification, monitoring and flexibility.

It may be helpful to make the following points about concentrated funding and partnership.

Concentrated funding

Fund resources will be concentrated on five priority objectives:

Objective 1. To promote the development of lagging Community regions whose GDP/head is lower than or close to 75 per cent of the Community average;

149

Objective 2.   Converting regions seriously affected by industrial decline (average rates of unemployment and industrial employment above the Community average, decline in industrial employment);

Objective 3.   Combating long–term unemployment (labour force aged over 25 and out of work for over 12 months);

Objective 4.   Facilitating the occupational integration of young people (job-seekers under 25);

Objective 5.   Helping to reform the common agricultural policy by:

        a)   adapting the structures of production, processing and marketing in agriculture and forestry;

        b)   fostering the development of particularly vulnerable rural areas with high levels of employment in agriculture, low agricultural earnings levels and low GDP/head.

The Objective 1 regions generally have a high rural component. Adapting agricultural structures (Objective 5a) will often mean targeting the preponderant sector of activity in a rural area. The Objective 5b areas are essentially rural. This means that rural development will benefit in several different ways from greater concentration in the utilisation of the Community's Structural Funds, which in any case will probably be reflected in the provision of more substantial financial resources in certain areas of the Community.

The reform of the structural funds involves a distinction between three geographical categories (see map on page 153) qualifying for Community rural development intervention on specific terms:

— *Structurally lagging regions* referred to in Objective 1 (30 per cent of the territory, 21.2 per cent of the population);

— *Vulnerable rural areas* referred to in Objective 5b (17.3 per cent of the territory and 5.1 per cent of the population);

— *Other rural areas* in the Community remaining eligible for general provisions available throughout the Community, particularly EAGGF measures to improve agricultural structures and training and possibly ESF assistance towards individual redeployment.

The first two categories of regions and areas eligible for more concentrated intervention represent nearly half of the Community territory and over one–quarter of its population.

In addition to the reform of the Structural Funds and the subsequent division of the Community into areas, the Community of course continues to encourage rural development throughout its territory via its other territorial policies.

Partnership

Partnership is the key principle in the Structural Funds reform insofar as it determines the implementation of the four other principles. Partnership derives from the need for Community intervention to be subsidiary to intervention by the other public partners.

Implementing partnership calls for close co–operation between the Commission (Community level) and the Member State (national, regional, local or other level), with all parties pursuing a common goal.

Partnership thereby introduces consultation from one level to another with a view to efficiency in division of labour and pooling of resources.

The emergence of the Community dimension in partnership for rural development not only opens up new prospects but holds out new challenges. Its significance lies in taking more account of European economic integration, and especially the benefits to economic agents of the completion of the internal market by 1993, in rural development intervention. One particular benefit will be greater coherence in rural development measures on either side of national frontiers. Rural development will be able to take more account of the Community's sectoral policy aims.

But paying systematic regard to the Community level in this partnership will set a real challenge for the former national and regional partners, in that the Community will now be an extra dimension in all their thinking.

Procedure, Timetable

The new Community approach towards rural development, especially for the regions and areas referred to in Objectives 1 and 5b, is now implemented to a set procedure with four successive stages:

a) Programmes, plans;
b) Community support frameworks;
c) Operational programmes;
d) Monitoring and evaluation.

The partnership principle should apply in each of these stages. It is particularly important at the monitoring and evaluation stage, for which special Monitoring Committees representing the leading partners will be set up.

This thoroughgoing reform of the Community's rural development stance and procedures came into force on 1st January 1989. It has been implemented gradually. Stages (a) and (b) have already put into effect for Objective 1 and very soon will be for Objectives 2, 3 and 4. For Objective 5 a longer lead time has proved necessary because:

For 5a   The underlying regulations needed to be adapted to the reform of the Funds. The EEC Council has recently adopted new provisions which will enter into force by the end of 1989.

For 5b   Eligible areas were defined in the spring of 1989 and the Member States concerned were notified in June. Development plans were formulated and transmitted to the Commission in late October. Work still in hand on formulating the Community support frameworks will be completed in April 1990.

The Single European Act and the regulations it has already prompted[2] have introduced the two new concepts of rural development and partnership into everyday Community language. The reform of the Community Structural Funds as an instrument with which to strengthen the socio-economic cohesion called for in the Single European Act is under way.

The new approach implies a change of habit and approach for public servants at three levels (regional, national and Community). Overcoming the challenges now facing those concerned with rural development will demand close and frank co-operation at every level.

As the reform proceeds, some adjustments will probably be necessary. Effective partnership will identify these while securing the essential degree of flexibility for the process in general.

NOTES AND REFERENCES

1. The Community has three Structural Funds:
    — The European Regional Development Fund (ERDF);
    — The European Social Fund (ESF);
    — The European Agricultural Guarantee and Guidance Fund (EAGGF Guidance Section).
    These three funds make grants.
    Other financial instruments concerned by the reform, in particular the European Investment Bank (EIB) make loans.
2. EEC Regulations No. 2052/88, 4253/88, 4254/88, 4255/88 and 4256/88 of the Council.

Table 1

Current indicative budget breakdown[1] for structural funds and priority objectives for the period 1989-1993

Billion Ecus[2]

Priority objective number	Budget per Fund 1988-1993					Total annual budget (All funds)	
	ERDF	ESF	EAGGF(0)	Total	%	1989	1993
1 CCA*	21.0	9.8	5.4	36.2		5.8	9.5
(reserve)				2.1	63		
2	5	2.2		7.2	12	1.0	1.6
3 et 4		7.4		7.4	12	1.2	1.9
5a			3.4	3.4	6	0.6	0.7
5b	1.0	0.5	1.3	2.8	5	0.3	0.9
Total for Priority Objectives[3]				59.1	98	8.9	14.6
Transitory measures and innovative activities	0.7	0.3	0.2	1.2	2	0.3	0.4
Total for Funds Amount[3]				60.3	100	9.2	15.0
%				100			

1. As of 1st December 1989.
2. Value: at 1989 prices.
3. The budget totals by Fund were not yet definitively fixed as of 1/12/89.
*   *Cadres communautaires d'appui* (community support frameworks).

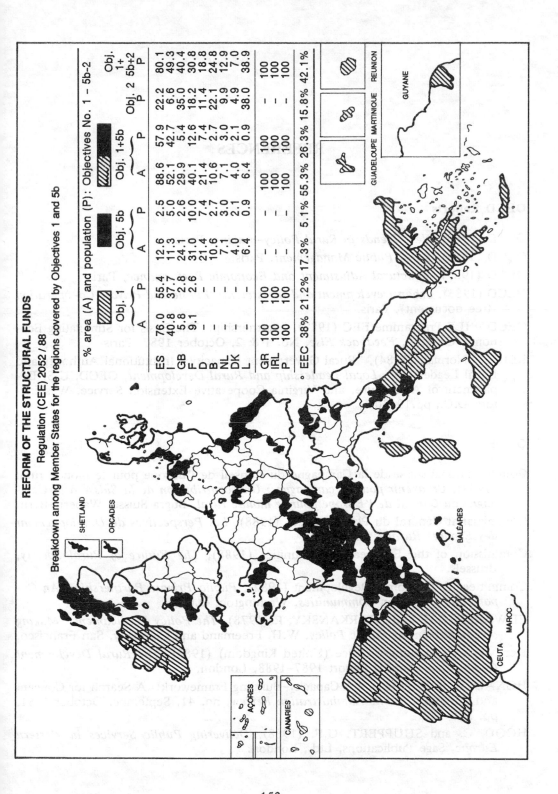

REFORM OF THE STRUCTURAL FUNDS

Regulation (CEE) 2052 / 88

Breakdown among Member States for the regions covered by Objectives 1 and 5b

% area (A) and population (P) : Objectives No. 1 – 5b-2

| | Obj. 1 | | Obj. 5b | | Obj. 1+5b | | Obj. 1+5b | | Obj. 2 | | Obj. 1+5b+2 | |
	A	P	A	P	A	P	A	P	A	P	A	P
ES	76.0	55.4	12.6	2.5	88.6	57.9			22.2		80.1	
I	40.8	37.7	11.3	5.0	52.1	42.7			6.6		49.3	
GB	5.8	2.8	24.1	2.6	29.9	5.4			35.0		40.4	
F	9.1	2.6	31.0	10.0	40.1	12.6			18.2		30.8	
D	–	–	21.4	7.4	21.4	7.4			11.4		18.8	
B	–	–	10.6	2.7	10.6	2.7			22.1		24.8	
NL	–	–	7.1	3.0	7.1	3.0			9.9		12.9	
DK	–	–	4.0	2.1	4.0	2.1			4.9		7.0	
L	–	–	6.4	0.9	6.4	0.9			38.0		38.9	
GR	100	100	–	–	100	100			–		100	
IRL	100	100	–	–	100	100			–		100	
P	100	100	–	–	100	100			–		100	
EEC	38%	21.2%	17.3%	5.1%	55.3%	26.3%		15.8%	42.1%			

SHETLAND
ORCADES
BALEARES
CEUTA
MAROC
AÇORES
CANARIES
GUADELOUPE MARTINIQUE REUNION
GUYANE

REFERENCES

OECD Reports

OECD (1988), *New Trends in Rural Policy-making*, Paris.

OECD (1986), *Rural Public Management*, Paris.

OECD (1987), *Structural Adjustment and Economic Performance,* Paris.

OECD (1983), *Urban Development and Investment: Public and Private Co-operation* (free document), Paris.

OECD – ILE Programme/EEC (1987), "Partnership: The Basis for Stimulating Economic Growth", *Feedback Else*, No. 1 & 2, October 1987, Paris.

REID, J. Norman (1984), "Rural Government Capacity: Institutional Authority and Local Leadership", *Local Leadership and Rural Development*, OECD, U.S. Department of Agriculture, and Virginia Cooperative Extension Service, Washington, D.C., pp.19–30.

Other

Comité national suisse de la Campagne du Conseil de l'Europe pour le monde rural (1989), *Un avenir pour la campagne : Une contribution de la Suisse à la Campagne du Conseil de l'Europe pour le monde rural*, Bugra Suisse, Wabern–Bern.

Commissariat Général du Plan (France) (1988), *Les Perspectives de Développement des Espaces Ruraux*, Paris.

Commission of the European Communities (1988), *The Future of Rural Society*, Brussels.

Committee for Economic Development (1982), *Public–Private Partnership: An Opportunity for Urban Communities*, Washington, D.C.

EDWARDS, G.C. and SHARKANSKY, I. (1978), *The Policy Predicament: Making and Implementing Public Policy*, W.H. Freemand and Company, San Francisco.

Her Majesty's Stationery Office (United Kingdom) (1988), *The Rural Development Commission*, Annual Report 1987–1988, London.

HONADLE, B.W. (1981), "A Capacity–Building Framework: A Search for Concept and Purpose", *Public Administration Review*, no. 41, September/October 1981, pp. 575–580.

HOOD, C. and SHUPPERT, G.F. (1988), *Delivering Public Services in Western Europe*, Sage Publications, Ltd., London.

JONES, C.O. (1977), *An Introduction to the Study of Public Policy*, 2nd edition, Duxbury Press, Wadsworth Publishing Company, Inc., Belmont, California.

KANTER, R.M. (1983), *The Change Masters: Innovation and Entrepreneurship in the American Corporation*, Simon and Schuster, New York.

KOENIG, L.W. (1986), *An Introduction to Public Policy*, Prentice–Hall, Englewood Cliffs, New Jersey.

Local Government and Regional Division, Department of Immigration and Ethnic Affairs (1987), *Australian Regional Developments. Country Centres Project*, Australian Government Publishing Service, Canberra.

Ministry of Agriculture (France), Direction de l'Espace Rural et de la Forêt (1987), *Où en sont les Chartes Intercommunales*, Paris.

Ministry of Agriculture (Netherlands) (1988), *The Land Development Act: An Outline*, The Hague.

Ministry of National Economy (Greece) and the Hellenic Agency for Local Development and Local Government (1988), *Contractual Policies for the Development of Rural Areas: The Planning Contract of Amvrakikos*, Athens.

OAKERSON, R. J. (1987), "Local Public Economies: Provision, Production, and Governance", *Intergovernmental Perspective*, no. 13, Summer/Fall 1987, pp. 20–25.

REGENS, J.L. (1988), "Institutional Co–ordination of Program Action", *International Journal of Public Administration*, no. 11 (2), pp. 135–154.

ROGERS, D.L. and WHETTEN, D.A. (1983), *Interorganizational Coordination: Theory, Research, and Implementation*, Iowa State University Press, Ames, Iowa.

SEREC (1985), *Rôle des animateurs dans les régions rurales et montagnardes*, Vissoie, Switzerland.

United States Department of Agriculture (1987), *Rural Economic Development in the 1980s: Preparing for the Future*, Washington, D.C.

WHERE TO OBTAIN OECD PUBLICATIONS
OÙ OBTENIR LES PUBLICATIONS DE L'OCDE

Argentina – Argentine
Carlos Hirsch S.R.L.
Galeria Güemes, Florida 165, 4° Piso
1333 Buenos Aires
Tel. 30.7122, 331.1787 y 331.2391
Telegram: Hirsch-Baires
Telex: 21112 UAPE-AR. Ref. s/2901
Telefax:(1)331-1787

Australia – Australie
D.A. Book (Aust.) Pty. Ltd.
648 Whitehorse Road (P.O. Box 163)
Vic. 3132   Tel. (03)873.4411
Telex: AA37911 DA BOOK
Telefax: (03)873.5679

Austria – Autriche
OECD Publications and Information Centre
4 Simrockstrasse
5300 Bonn (Germany)   Tel. (0228)21.60.45
Telex: 8 86300 Bonn
Telefax: (0228)26.11.04
Gerold & Co.
Graben 31
Wien I   Tel. (0222)533.50.14

Belgium – Belgique
Jean De Lannoy
Avenue du Roi 202
B-1060 Bruxelles
Tel. (02)538.51.69/538.08.41
Telex: 63220 Telefax: (02)538.08.41

Canada
Renouf Publishing Company Ltd.
1294 Algoma Road
Ottawa, Ont. K1B 3W8 Tel. (613)741.4333
Telex: 053-4783 Telefax: (613)741.5439
Stores:
61 Sparks Street
Ottawa, Ont. K1P 5R1 Tel. (613)238.8985
211 Yonge Street
Toronto, Ont. M5B 1M4 Tel. (416)363.3171
Federal Publications
165 University Avenue
Toronto, ON M5H 3B9   Tel. (416)581.1552
Telefax: (416)581.1743
Les Publications Fédérales
1185 rue de l'Université
Montréal, PQ H3B 1R7 Tel. (514)954-1633
Les Éditions La Liberté Inc.
3020 Chemin Sainte-Foy
Sainte-Foy, P.Q. G1X 3V6
Tel. (418)658.3763
Telefax: (418)658.3763

Denmark – Danemark
Munksgaard Export and Subscription Service
35, Norre Sogade, P.O. Box 2148
DK-1016 Kobenhavn K
Tel. (45 33)12.85.70
Telex: 19431 MUNKS DK
Telefax: (45 33)12.93.87

Finland – Finlande
Akateeminen Kirjakauppa
Keskuskatu 1, P.O. Box 128
00100 Helsinki   Tel. (358 0)12141
Telex: 125080 Telefax: (358 0)121.4441

France
OECD/OCDE
Mail Orders/Commandes par correspon-
dance:
2 rue André-Pascal
75775 Paris Cedex 16   Tel. (1)45.24.82.00
Bookshop/Librairie:
33, rue Octave-Feuillet
75016 Paris   Tel. (1)45.24.81.67
                           (1)45.24.81.81
Telex: 620 160 OCDE
Telefax: (33-1)45.24.85.00
Librairie de l'Université
12a, rue Nazareth
13602 Aix-en-Provence   Tel. 42.26.18.08

Germany – Allemagne
OECD Publications and Information Centre
4 Simrockstrasse
5300 Bonn   Tel. (0228)21.60.45
Telex: 8 86300 Bonn
Telefax: (0228)26.11.04

Greece – Grèce
Librairie Kauffmann
28 rue du Stade
105 64 Athens   Tel. 322.21.60
Telex: 218187 LIKA Gr

Hong Kong
Swindon Book Co. Ltd
13-15 Lock Road
Kowloon, Hong Kong   Tel. 366.80.31
Telex: 50.441 SWIN HX
Telefax: 739.49.75

Iceland – Islande
Mal Mog Menning
Laugavegi 18, Postholf 392
121 Reykjavik   Tel. 15199/24240

India – Inde
Oxford Book and Stationery Co.
Scindia House
New Delhi 110001   Tel. 331.5896/5308
Telex: 31 61990 AM IN
Telefax: (11)332.5993
17 Park Street
Calcutta 700016   Tel. 240832

Indonesia – Indonésie
Pdii-Lipi
P.O. Box 269/JKSMG/88
Jakarta12790   Tel. 583467
Telex: 62 875

Ireland – Irlande
TDC Publishers – Library Suppliers
12 North Frederick Street
Dublin 1   Tel. 744835/749677
Telex: 33530 TDCP EI Telefax : 748416

Italy – Italie
Libreria Commissionaria Sansoni
Via Benedetto Fortini, 120/10
Casella Post. 552
50125 Firenze   Tel. (055)645415
Telex: 570466 Telefax: (39.55)641257
Via Bartolini 29
20155 Milano   Tel. 365083
La diffusione delle pubblicazioni OCSE viene
assicurata dalle principali librerie ed anche
da:
Editrice e Libreria Herder
Piazza Montecitorio 120
00186 Roma   Tel. 679.4628
Telex: NATEL I 621427
Libreria Hoepli
Via Hoepli 5
20121 Milano   Tel. 865446
Telex: 31.33.95 Telefax: (39.2)805.2886
Libreria Scientifica
Dott. Lucio de Biasio "Aeiou"
Via Meravigli 16
20123 Milano   Tel. 807679
Telefax: 800175

Japan – Japon
OECD Publications and Information Centre
Landic Akasaka Building
2-3-4 Akasaka, Minato-ku
Tokyo 107   Tel. 586.2016
Telefax: (81.3)584.7929

Korea – Corée
Kyobo Book Centre Co. Ltd.
P.O. Box 1658, Kwang Hwa Moon
Seoul   Tel. (REP)730.78.91
Telex: 735.0030

**Malaysia/Singapore –
Malaisie/Singapour**
University of Malaya Co-operative Bookshop
Ltd.
P.O. Box 1127, Jalan Pantai Baru 59100
Kuala Lumpur
Malaysia   Tel. 756.5000/756.5425
Telefax: 757.3661
Information Publications Pte. Ltd.
Pei-Fu Industrial Building
24 New Industrial Road No. 02-06
Singapore 1953   Tel. 283.1786/283.1798
Telefax: 284.8875

Netherlands – Pays-Bas
SDU Uitgeverij
Christoffel Plantijnstraat 2
Postbus 20014
2500 EA's-Gravenhage   Tel. (070)78.99.11
Voor bestellingen: Tel. (070)78.98.80
Telex: 32486 stdru Telefax: (070)47.63.51

New Zealand –Nouvelle-Zélande
Government Printing Office
Customer Services
P.O. Box 12-411
Freepost 10-050
Thorndon, Wellington
Tel. 0800 733-406   Telefax: 04 499-1733

Norway – Norvège
Narvesen Info Center – NIC
Bertrand Narvesens vei 2
P.O. Box 6125 Etterstad
0602 Oslo 6
Tel. (02)67.83.10/(02)68.40.20
Telex: 79668 NIC N Telefax: (02)68.19.01

Pakistan
Mirza Book Agency
65 Shahrah Quaid-E-Azam
Lahore 3   Tel. 66839
Telex: 44886 UBL PK. Attn: MIRZA BK

Portugal
Livraria Portugal
Rua do Carmo 70-74
1117 Lisboa Codex   Tel. 347.49.82/3/4/5

**Singapore/Malaysia
Singapour/Malaisie**
See "Malaysia/Singapore"
Voir "Malaisie/Singapour"

Spain – Espagne
Mundi-Prensa Libros S.A.
Castello 37, Apartado 1223
Madrid 28001   Tel. (91) 431.33.99
Telex: 49370 MPLI Telefax: 575.39.98
Libreria Internacional AEDOS
Consejo de Ciento 391
08009 –Barcelona   Tel. (93) 301-86-15
Telefax: 575.39.98

Sweden – Suède
Fritzes Fackboksföretaget
Box 16356, S 103 27 STH
Regeringsgatan 12
DS Stockholm   Tel. (08)23.89.00
Telex: 12387 Telefax: (08)20.50.21
Subscription Agency/Abonnements:
Wennergren-Williams AB
Box 30004
104 25 Stockholm   Tel. (08)54.12.00
Telex: 19937 Telefax: (08)50.82.86

Switzerland – Suisse
OECD Publications and Information Centre
4 Simrockstrasse
5300 Bonn (Germany)   Tel. (0228)21.60.45
Telex: 8 86300 Bonn
Telefax: (0228)26.11.04
Librairie Payot
6 rue Grenus
1211 Genève 11   Tel. (022)731.89.50
Telex: 28356
Maditec S.A.
Ch. des Palettes 4
1020 Renens/Lausanne Tel. (021)635.08.65
Telefax: (021)635.07.80
United Nations Bookshop/Librairie des Na-
tions-Unies
Palais des Nations
1211 Genève 10
Tel. (022)734.60.11 (ext. 48.72)
Telex: 289696 (Attn: Sales)
Telefax: (022)733.98.79

Taïwan – Formose
Good Faith Worldwide Int'l. Co. Ltd.
9th Floor, No. 118, Sec. 2
Chung Hsiao E. Road
Taipei   Tel. 391.7396/391.7397
Telefax: (02) 394.9176

Thailand – Thalande
Suksit Siam Co. Ltd.
1715 Rama IV Road, Samyan
Bangkok 5   Tel. 251.1630

Turkey – Turquie
Kültur Yayinlari Is–Türk Ltd. Sti.
Atatürk Bulvari No. 191/Kat. 21
Kavaklidere/Ankara   Tel. 25.07.60
Dolmabahce Cad. No. 29
Besiktas/Istanbul   Tel. 160.71.88
Telex: 43482B

United Kingdom – Royaume-Uni
H.M. Stationery Office
Gen. enquiries   Tel. (071) 873 0011
Postal orders only:
P.O. Box 276, London SW8 5DT
Personal Callers HMSO Bookshop
49 High Holborn, London WC1V 6HB
Telex: 297138 Telefax: 071.873.8463
Branches at: Belfast, Birmingham, Bristol,
Edinburgh, Manchester

United States – États-Unis
OECD Publications and Information Centre
2001 L Street N.W., Suite 700
Washington, D.C. 20036-4095
Tel. (202)785.6323
Telex: 440245 WASHINGTON D.C.
Telefax: (202)785.0350

Venezuela
Libreria del Este
Avda F. Miranda 52, Aptdo. 60337
Edificio Galipan
Caracas 106
Tel. 951.1705/951.2307/951.1297
Telegram: Libreste Caracas

Yugoslavia – Yougoslavie
Jugoslovenska Knjiga
Knez Mihajlova 2, P.O. Box 36
Beograd   Tel. 621.992
Telex: 12466 jk bgd

Orders and inquiries from countries where
Distributors have not yet been appointed
should be sent to: OECD Publications
Service, 2 rue André-Pascal, 75775 Paris
Cedex 16.
Les commandes provenant de pays où
l'OCDE n'a pas encore désigné de dis-
tributeur devraient être adressées à : OCDE,
Service des Publications, 2, rue André-
Pascal, 75775 Paris Cedex 16.

OECD PUBLICATIONS 2, rue André-Pascal 75775 PARIS CEDEX 16
PRINTED IN FRANCE
(42 90 02 1) ISBN 92-64-13380-1 - No. 45177 1990

3/90